# THE EVANGELIZING CATHOLIC

## A PRACTICAL HANDBOOK FOR REACHING OUT

by

### Frank P. DeSiano, C.S.P.
### President of the Paulist Fathers

PAULIST PRESS
New York / Mahwah, N.J.

NIHIL OBSTAT: Frank J. Caggiano, S.T.D.
Censor of Books

IMPRIMATUR: Thomas V. Daily, D.D.
Bishop of Brooklyn

Brooklyn, New York    April 13, 1998

Library of Congress Cataloging-in-Publication Data

DeSiano, Frank P.
The evangelizing Catholic : a practical handbook for reaching out /
by Frank P. DeSiano.
        p.   cm.
Includes bibliographical references.
ISBN 0-8091-3836-0  (alk. paper)
1. Catholic Church–Doctrines–Handbooks, manuals, etc.  2. Evangelistic
work–Handbooks, manuals, etc.  I. Title.
BX2347.4.D474   1998
266′.2–DC21
98-38276
CIP

Cover design by Nighthawk Design

Interior design by Joseph E. Petta

Typeset in 11/14 Garamond

Published by Paulist Press
997 Macarthur Boulevard
Mahwah, New Jersey 07430

www.paulistpress.com

Printed and bound in the
United States of America

# Dedication

This little practical handbook for Catholic evangelization is dedicated to those thousands of Catholics—laypersons, religious and clergy—who have developed a commitment to evangelization and have become part of a concerted effort to help deepen the Catholic faith and spread its Good News.

*May Christ Jesus, who alone is our Good News, intensify your dedication and bring you the abundant blessings of God in the Holy Spirit. Amen.*

# Table of Contents

# Foreword

For over a quarter of a century, I have been a priest in the Paulist Fathers. This has meant that my priestly ministry has been inevitably intertwined with evangelization, even though that word did not start percolating in Catholic circles until a few years after my ordination, with the issuing of *On Evangelization in the Modern World,* Paul VI's brilliant response to the 1974 Synod of Bishops.

While I have been thinking about evangelization most of my life, in 1987 the Paulists were kind enough to let me go "whole hog" into this ministry, leading me to devote a considerable number of years working with parishes in the development of evangelization teams and the design of evangelization ministry.

As a result of this "whole hog" experience, I am aware that when it comes to evangelization, for most parishes, the truth comes down to this: "The spirit is willing but the parish doesn't know what to do." This is even truer of individual Catholics who have a profound and powerful grasp of the Gospel (really it's the other way around: the Gospel has a profound hold on them) but who feel so reluctant to share faith or so at a loss when the opportunity comes to express faith to another.

That's why I've written this little "handbook," which is not a collection of recipes but a little guide to open up the "how to" in evangelization, in two particular areas: (1) in the personal lives of Catholics and (2) in the ministries of parishes that wish to "reach out" in specific ways. As a result, this little book will not cover all the areas of evangelization, but focus on some outreach techniques that parishes can use with a variety of objectives—to reach unchurched people, to call to inactive Catholics, to organize particular programs.

My hope is that Catholics, using this book and many other resources, will find a way to exercise the powerful baptismal commission that Jesus has given them by the outpouring of his Spirit and the preaching of his Word.

The secret to sharing faith is not so impossible or so invisible that evangelization should be such a difficult labor for so many of us Catholics. The secret consists of what Christ has already given to us and what we, Sunday after Sunday, celebrate in his love.

# Chapter 1

---

# PRELIMINARY CONSIDERATIONS

Let's start with a shocker: evangelization is not any easier for us than it was for the early Christians.

This shocking realization comes not because of the clear evidence of how difficult evangelization seems to be for contemporary Catholics. Rather, we are shocked to see how the New Testament, through various hints, gives the same impression about the earliest followers of Jesus.

Look, for example, at the parable of the sower and the seed, a parable so important that it leads the list of those recorded by the Gospel of Mark and the Gospel of Matthew puts it at the start of the chapter in which many of the parables of Jesus are collected, chapter 13.

The parable seems simple—all parables are supposed to seem simple. Christ paints a clear image, that of someone throwing seed here and there. Christ follows up this simple image—one that people in his day probably saw in field after field at planting time—with a point-by-point narration of the result.

And those results are not particularly encouraging.

Seed goes here and there, but only some of it bears fruit. The other seed seems wasted, falling on hard ground, falling among thorns, falling onto thin soil. So much wasted effort, effort that the early Christians saw in those who took on their way of life, only to abandon it because of superficiality, because of the risks and costs of Christian living, or because they just loved money more.

Even the seed that does produce a yield has its hint of disappointments: only some of it yields "a hundredfold." The rest brings less, some considerably less.

### "It Was Easier Back Then"

Clearly this parable, and so many of the other parables, echo the evangelizing situation of the early Christians. It provides for us sobering information for we often think that evangelization had to be easier for those early Christians, so fresh in their experience of Jesus, so flush with miracles and other astonishing witnesses to faith, so intense in their faith.

We always seem to think about many past eras of the Church as somewhat more adept at evangelization than our own—holy monks in the desert, or wandering monks in northern Europe, or crusaders filled with hope, or followers of St. Francis and St. Dominic freely bringing about Christian renewal as they wandered their neighborhoods. Our minds get filled with fervent Jesuits converting thousands in Latin America or even far-off India, or religious communities that safaried deep into Africa to bring about the astonishing number of conversions to Christianity that occurred in the twentieth century.

They all seemed to have it so easy, but this makes it seem so much harder for us. We just don't have their magic, do we?

Of course we also know of the stories of the martyrs whose deaths looked like defeat, of the lonely journeys and frustrating disappointments of missionaries through the ages, of the tentative hold the faith always seems to have in any culture, even some of the most passionately Christian cultures just a few decades ago, but still, in our imaginations, our efforts in evangelization always seem weaker and more difficult.

## Unenthusiastic Catholics

Perhaps evangelization is colored with greater romance when it seems "far away" and "ancient," because when we look at today's religious world, especially in the United States, we see a large, institutional Catholic Church with pockets of great fervor in the midst of an enormous field of inertia. Evangelization seems hard for us because we seem to be so unexcitable.

What are we to do with all these Catholics who appear—even among those diminishing numbers who regularly attend church—so unenthused? Of course we know that thousands of Catholics have become part of small Christian sharing groups and thousands more have gotten involved in the study of the Scriptures or highly charged prayer groups. But most practicing Catholics just "go to church," putting their donation in the collection basket, volunteering for one or another kind of worthwhile activity if they feel the urge (or the guilt), faithfully trying to do "what is right" according to current admonitions.

This large number of people, now either very suburban or very ethnic, does not give the impression of being willing to take up the cry of evangelization. Modern Catholics seem more into survival, to "hanging on," to being faithful.

How, we wonder, will today's Catholics ever become an evangelizing Church? Is it even possible, given today's society and the dispositions of Catholics, to conceive of what "an evangelizing Catholic" might look like?

## Hopeful Signs

Most probably it always looked this way, throughout Christian history. We easily remember heroic figures or special eras of history. But it is hard to have a memory of the "ordinary Christian" that formed the background of all these twenty centuries of Christian life. That is why the parable of the sower, or St. Paul's impassioned letter to his stubborn Corinthian congregation, the complaints about the "laxness" of Christian life after it became publicly acceptable in the time of Constantine, the images of the "Dark Ages" plagued with superstition and ignorance or of the pre-Reformation Church with its scandals and convenient compromises, or the times of anticlericalism in France and Italy, even the rather weak practice of faith three or four generations back in our own families—that is why these sobering images can help put our present concerns into a larger context.

In reality, it probably always looked bleak. Christians probably always look lax compared to the ideals set before them. Evangelization always looks difficult, if not impossible, given the state of the Church.

That's the cynical view, and it helps a bit.

But we don't have to settle just for cynicism's colder consolation. Because in our own day, even as we survey the field of "unenthusiastic Catholics," we see things stirring. Parish after parish is receiving adult converts to the faith every year, some of them in great numbers. Diocese after diocese has conducted workshops for clergy and laypeople about evangelization. Several dioceses have made evangelization their primary goal; some of them even have evangelization teams formed in a large percentage of their parishes. The United States bishops' *Go and Make Disciples: A Plan and Strategy for Catholic Evangelization in the United States* (November, 1992) has been read and studied by scores of thousands. The always elusive goal of trying to reach formerly active or nominal Catholics also seems to be picking up steam as Catholics begin to take reconciliation as a central ministry in their parishes.

Something is happening, in spite of how hard it seems. The sower has a sackful of seed and has started to toss it around.

## A Little Help

What hinders much evangelizing activity is the feeling that "we Catholics don't know what to do." Again and again parishioners and priests ask for "something to help us evangelize, to help us get started." While *Go and Make Disciples* was issued by the bishops precisely as an indispensable aid to "get started" (it is, after all, a plan and strategy), Catholics still ask for more.

This little book is intended to fill a gap—the need for a practical little "handbook" to help "get started." We Catholics have had enough practical experience in attempting to evangelize over these past few decades that some principles and approaches can be outlined.

Beware, however, of anyone who hands out "recipes" for evangelization. Such "automatic programs" with "cut-and-dried approaches" that "really work" can be little more than fantasies. While some notions about marketing or communications bear on evangelization, by and large evangelization has always been, and will always be, a pastoral activity that arises deep from within the Holy Spirit's mysterious action in our lives.

As we look at some preliminary considerations, the truth of the "no recipe" reality to evangelization will become clear.

What is "tried and true" about evangelization is the faith behind it, the powerful daily faith that makes individual Catholics and Catholic parishes mindful of the great gift of faith they have received and of those millions whose lives are emptier because they have no faith. Such a perspective does not give rise to recipes but to hopes—and to the energy to begin making those hopes real. No one packages that energy; they incarnate it, again and again, in many different situations through which God's Word is heard by others in welcome and acceptance.

Our preliminary considerations have to go beyond the current state of evangelization and what resources might be supplied to help. Before we can look at evangelization personally and in our parishes, we need to think about important

Catholic assumptions about evangelization—discipleship, encounter, the peer dimension of evangelization—and some basic information about the "what and the how" of this ministry. After we have done that, we can, in chapter 2, explore possibilities in personal evangelization.

## DISCIPLESHIP

Evangelization cannot happen unless disciples do it.

Between the fact that all Christians are called to discipleship and the observation that most Christians,when they think of disciples, think only of "special people," lies one of the great chasms of Christian life.

Me, a disciple?

Cannot be.

Yet it is precisely "me," with all my gifts and limitations, that Christ has made a disciple. And it is only when we come to consider ourselves as disciples that we can begin to get a handle on the gifts Christ has given each of his followers—gifts that equip them to evangelize.

Catholics so readily think of themselves only as "parishioners" who "follow the directions" of their pastors. This attitude causes such caution, such hesitation, that we rarely feel the simple strength needed to share our own personal experiences with others or to invite someone who is in need to approach Christ more closely.

We huddle in our parishes, bury our faces in our missalettes, organize our life according to certain activities that make us feel comfortable, and believe that salvation primarily is about our own souls.

But when we start living as the disciples we are, then the wall of caution with which we surround ourselves will start to disintegrate.

What might be some of the implications of being a disciple?

## Disciples in God

Jesus was a master teacher. The fact that even today we can stand at Mass and be utterly startled by the words of the Gospel reveals the plain force of the teachings of Jesus. Whether through parables, elaborate discourses, small pithy phrases or sharp rejoinders, Jesus had the ability to cut through to the essence of an idea and, in the process, to cut through to the core of the human heart. He made people think. He makes us think.

Most of all, he makes us think about God because no one can be a disciple without constantly plumbing the fullness of God. God is the mystery that grounds us, surrounds us and leads us forward. God tugs at our consciousness, begs for our attention, promises untold wisdom and challenges the shallowness of our lives.

Prayer is the way we acknowledge, grow in and respond to this consciousness about God. Prayer characterized the life of Jesus and his disciples more than anything else. A quick read of the Sermon on the Mount (Mt 5–7) brings home the constantly profound level of prayer Jesus enjoined—and the consequent attitudes of trust and faith that emerge from that prayer.

To write at the head of every topic and every section of this manual, "Of course, you must pray for this" or, "Without prayer, evangelization cannot happen," would make for boring reading. So the reader must constantly supply these basic truths: absolutely every fruit that evangelization will bring about begins in prayer, is sustained through prayer and will be celebrated in the prayer of thankful praise.

Two levels of prayer are essential: (1) personal prayer that both connects the disciple to the mystery of God and makes concrete persons and occasions its focus; and (2) prayer of the Christian community at Mass and other gatherings of prayer.

## *Disciples for Others*

Beyond the fundamental starting point of prayer, another dimension of discipleship involves our relationship with others: the disciple does not live for him- or herself. The disciple lives for others.

Much modern religion, particularly in the United States, has the point of faith backwards. Moderns construe religion as this great personal awareness that enhances our personal lives. It emphasizes the faith, joy and peace that come from faith and then almost lulls the believer to be locked up in a kind of self-enclosed inner space. The kinds of prayer encouraged in much modern faith, even when done with others, often seem self-absorbed.

What happened to the restlessness of Paul, this intense disciple who would collapse if he did not get to preach the Gospel (1 Cor 9:16)? We see Paul narrating the sufferings that he underwent while spreading the Good News; but was not the greatest concern he mentions his "constant anxiety for the churches," that is, for others (2 Cor 11:22–28)?

The Church, in the cycle of readings after Easter when the proclamation of the Good News echoes freshly in our assemblies, reads most of all from the writings of John, both the Gospel and the First Letter. The thrust of these readings comes down to one basic thought: our love for God is verified in our love for each other, in accomplishing the commandment of Christ in our lives, that we "love one another as I have loved you" (Jn 13:34, among other passages).

We Catholics have to learn how to resist the natural tendency to think of the Gospel as something that happens primarily in the inner sanctums of the heart or the stained-glass sanctuaries of our church buildings. Such "inner sanctum" notions are totally foreign to the New Testament. The Gospel happens in our daily life, in the commitment that we have for the bringing of God's Kingdom—with its demands for justice, peace and universal love—to greater actuality in the world.

## Disciples in Community

Yet a third dimension of discipleship touches essentially on what it means to be followers of Jesus: that we are disciples together, with others, as members of his community, the Church.

This challenges yet another modern distortion about faith, the idea that we can be "believers but not belongers," to use the phrase of the famous sociologist of American religion Wade Clark Roofe (*A Generation of Believers,* HarperCollins, 1993). According to his studies of the religious lives of "baby boomers," about a third of church members never strayed from their practice; about a quarter strayed but then returned. The remaining percentage, greater than 45 percent, drifted away from their church, drift from church to church or just absolve themselves from any consideration about church. For a large number of these people, the tag "believers but not belongers" fits perfectly.

While church attendance may not be the most accurate measure of faith, it does undeniably speak to the social dimension of faith, our ability to see our faith as essentially involved in the relationships that we have with others. In no phase of our personal lives do we imagine it is possible to grow without the support, challenge and just plain contact that comes from others. Yet so many of us imagine that this is possible when it comes to faith. No wonder our society, for all its religious babble, never seems completely grounded in faith.

The New Testament suffers from no such individualism. The Gospel of John lays down clearly the importance of God's Word in our lives, as well as the need we have to "feed upon" the body of the Lord. (See Jn 6:41–51.) Jesus gathers the twelve apostles precisely as a sign of his gathering of "all the tribes" of Israel (Mt 19:28). Paul founds congregation after congregation and works to tie each together into one understanding of God's gracious mercy—and also into common behaviors that will sustain the faith of that congregation.

If we think it's possible to read the New Testament and not stumble across the intrinsic importance of the community's faith at every step, then we are simply misreading the New Testament.

Because God calls us to be disciples through, in and for community, discipleship cannot happen without church.

## Goals and Discipleship

The role of discipleship—in its prayerful consciousness of God, in its community and its service of others—supports the three goals that basically shape the pastoral activity that we call evangelization. These goals, elaborated by the bishops of the United States in *Go and Make Disciples,* expand the basic notion of evangelization that Pope Paul VI developed in his pastoral letter *On Evangelization in the Modern World* (December, 1975) in three clear directions:

1. Evangelization calls for the continued renewal of the believer and the Church so that we will have the enthusiasm for our faith that is needed to share that faith with others.

2. Evangelization calls for welcoming and inviting others to get to know Jesus in his saving message and in his Church.

3. Evangelization intensifies the impact of our faith on our world, on the dignity of the human person and the importance of the family, so that Christ may continue to transform our modern society.

The renewal of ourselves in faith, the reaching out to others and the service of the world all reinforce the perspective of those who, as disciples, are called to follow Jesus with all their hearts.

# ENCOUNTER

Once we become aware of our discipleship, then we can begin to see how faith occurs in the everyday encounters of our lives.

One of the dangers of talking about different "techniques" or "methods" of evangelization, as we will do in this handbook, is that it might feed that part of our modern mind that thinks of "strategies" and "methodologies" that will, almost automatically, make things happen.

One cannot go to a conference on evangelization without people asking for presentations about "things that really work," as if, with good American know-how and a strong can-do attitude, evangelization were a process of applying tried-and-true techniques to situations and—presto!—getting guaranteed results.

Much as we all want to believe in technique, and much as technique is important on some level—certainly, bad technique can hinder the progress of evangelization—the truth is that evangelization, before it is a method or strategy, is a human encounter.

Once a group of parishioners went visiting door-to-door, all the male visitors dressed in shirt and tie, and the women in simple dresses. One particular lady eyed two male parishioners and did her best to completely evade them. Finally, she made a turn that landed her directly in their path. When they introduced themselves as from the neighboring Catholic parish, she breathed a sigh of relief. "Thank God you are Catholics," she said. "I thought you were Jehovah's Witnesses." (This might be a good reason to drop the ties when we go visiting!)

Maybe she thought Catholics were harmless. But she clearly thought that the technique of home visiting, in the way it is regularly practiced by Jehovah's Witnesses, would be of no benefit to her. Why? Because it's hard to feel that people who are so adamantly wedded to one method, with one preordained result, really care about the individual person. Undoubtedly most sincere Jehovah's Witnesses care deeply about those they will meet. But maybe the method gets in the way.

Gets in the way of what? Of truly encountering the other.

## The Example of Christ

For all the times we think of Jesus preaching to the crowds, it's those powerful one-to-one moments with others that stand out most in our imagination. Jesus talking to the Samaritan woman at the well. Jesus with Jairus, whose daughter had died. Jesus and the woman who could not stop bleeding. Jesus and Matthew. Jesus and Peter when the fish are caught and Peter becomes a disciple.

We even remember his intimate moments with friends, imagining him often at table with Martha, Mary and Lazarus. Or taking the three apostles, Peter, James and John, aside to drive home a point more clearly. Or praying with the women who followed him so faithfully—who were the only ones to follow him on the last steps of his life. Spiritually, we are probably most envious of these most intimate moments.

Jesus, in these meetings with others, seems to us so approachable, so human, so vivid and real because Jesus acts in these situations with the most instinctual and deepest trait of our human natures: the ability to encounter another as a brother or sister. Nothing distinguishes human life so powerfully as our capacity to have our lives opened up by those whom we truly meet and engage with.

This goes well beyond the "chitchat" mode of much of our banter, in which we have ways of socializing with people but not truly engaging them as brothers or sisters. Chitchat works for acquaintances, for coworkers who remain only that, or incidental golfing companions or those with whom we might go shopping. We chitchat in front of the TV or before a ball game begins. This is contact and this is distance at the same time. The encounter of another human being, however, does more than establish a neutral base or fill time spent with another. It involves us in the lives of another, and involves that other in our lives as well.

Jesus shows that encounter has the power to change people. It engages them in such a way that it invites them on a journey that might well make their lives different. The Samaritan woman at the well gets so excited because of the One who "told me everything that I did" that she must run to her townspeople with news of this man she so marvelously met (Jn 4:39). However we conceive Mary Magdalene—and some of our ideas about her truly are off the wall—her life changed when she met Jesus (Lk 8:1-2).

Encounter changes people because it touches people on the level of love and care–such love and care that people who otherwise feel afraid, stuck, shoved aside or smug come to see new possibilities for themselves. New ways of living. New ways of thinking. New ways of loving because they have felt another's liberating love.

Jesus was that way. The disciples of Jesus can do no better than to follow his approach.

## *Encounter Opens Lives*

Encounter is adventure. It flows from the human adventure of living, of coming to be who we are, of always being unfinished, of always needing to grow and change. No true change happens completely alone. When our life changes with the presence and influence of others, they accompany us on our adventure, they become part of our story, our history.

So encounter has to be open-ended since life itself is open-ended. It has to be based in trust since we can grow only in trust. And it has to be mutual on some real level since we otherwise feel manipulated and used. Even when important persons were in no way our peers (say, teachers, religious leaders or parents), we still felt, in spite of the inequality, an openness to the soul of that person. We felt how they cared for us, how they let us into their lives even as we let them into our lives.

Because each person has a history that will continue to unfold even more into the future, encounter means that we cannot predetermine what our meetings will amount to. We might briefly remember the significant people in our own lives, how we met them, how much we changed as a result of knowing them, the ongoing influence they exert on our lives and, as important, the ongoing influence they let us have in their lives. Our involvement with them is like a journey of discovery.

Evangelization takes place as encounter. It involves two or more people engaging in open trust on the basis of their genuine care for each other. This encounter happens in faith.

Evangelization is a spiritual encounter in the adventure of faith. But it begins in human encounter, in the caring we have for another, our willingness to let people into our lives, our responsiveness to their invitation to be part of their lives, and the trusting love that is the essential possibility for this kind of human interchange. The disciple does not separate human encounter from spiritual encounter because he or she keeps spirituality at the center of life. The disciple does not use spirituality to structure every encounter because true human sharing is not structured and true spirituality always shines through. The disciple does not make some predetermined outcome the basis of encounter; rather the disciple trusts the Spirit of God to bring about human and saving fullness in accord with the uniqueness of each person.

No one can evangelize unless he or she is willing to encounter. Every evangelization technique or every large-scale evangelization drive stands or falls on the willingness of people to encounter others as human beings in the adventure of their lives.

When people feel the care of Jesus in our care, then our message may begin to get home.

We need to remind ourselves of the truth of human

encounter (how God's grace builds on the "nature" of human meeting) at every step of the evangelization process. Otherwise it becomes abstract, distant and contrived.

God meets us in history, both personal and global. So without a meeting, a true encounter, how can God be found?

# THE "PEER" DIMENSION OF EVANGELIZATION

The fundamental ideas of discipleship and encounter lead to another essential point of evangelization: the Gospel spreads from person to person, mostly in a peer relationship.

We might, for example, look at Jesus' sending forth of the seventy-two disciples in the Gospel of Luke (10:1 ff.). After he instructs them about various matters—we'll look again at some of those instructions in the pages ahead—he tells them to greet people and wish them peace. When one's greeting of peace is returned, then the Gospel can begin to be spread.

In other words, there is a relationship built upon a give-and-take exchange of peace, of association, of friendship, which undergirds the growth of God's Good News.

Somewhat analogously, we can recall Jesus' seemingly strange instruction to his disciples: "Go first among the lost sheep of the house of Israel" (Mt 10:6). We scratch our heads.... Didn't Jesus want the Gospel to go to everyone? Wasn't it Jesus who went to such "pagan" towns as Caesarea Philippi or to the cities of the Decapolis?

Yet maybe all Jesus is teaching his followers is the simple and obvious rule: begin close to home, begin with those around you, begin with your peers.

## *Family Are Not Peers*

No evangelization ministry looms more pressingly in the hearts of most Catholics than outreach to inactive Catholics, those millions of people who call themselves "Catholic" but in effect have no real involvement in the Church and, for all practical purposes, no effective life of faith.

When Catholics hear the term *evangelization,* they cringe a little bit (though thankfully less than they used to) because this term has become a staple of Catholic language in the last three decades. But when Catholics hear that evangelization means doing something about welcoming and reconciling inactive Catholics, their hearts get stirred.

They respond positively because they can immediately think of Catholics who have stopped practicing their faith, and this stoppage of living the faith has caused a great sense of pain, of loss.

The paradoxical thing in all of this is that when Catholics think of these inactive Catholics, they think of the very people they are *least* likely to be able to help. They think of family members. Parents think of children. Children think of parents. We imagine cousins, aunts, grandchildren: all these blood relationships whose bonds are tested by a seeming absence of faith.

Yet when we reflect on the situation pastorally, our relatives are the last people we are likely to be able to reach, at least in any direct sense. Why? Wouldn't it seem clearly the case that we should get our own "households" in order? That if faith cannot be shared between relatives, then it surely cannot be shared with anyone?

Yet a little analysis reveals why this seemingly obvious strategy is wrong. After all, the connection that relatives have between each other has its historical plusses and minuses. Parents have raised, loved and also nagged their children for decades. Brothers have palled around with brothers, and have also fought with them. Sisters have shared secrets, and also kept them. These very dynamics between relatives complicate what it means for one to talk to another about something as sensitive as the practice of faith. We can easily imagine the one brother, who all his life felt bullied by his older brother, telling that older brother to get lost when something sensitive arises. "Stop bullying me" would be the ingrained response.

Thinking about relatives is *not* thinking about peers because peers have more or less equal and uncluttered relationships. Instead of immediately lunging ahead toward our children or siblings, "thinking peers" means thinking about coworkers, friends, and neighbors who may well be able to hear our message without the historically personal distractions that so often come with family life.

## The Power of Peers

The New Testament inclines us to think "hierarchically" in, for example, the book of Acts, where we see Peter making his orations to his fellow Jews or Paul proudly giving his speech on the Areopagus in Athens. These talks, stylized by Luke, represent fundamental approaches used by the early Church to proclaim the Good News of God. The stylization makes us think that evangelization is something like giving speeches to others, preferably on a one-to-many basis. In other words, we think that evangelization means the "preacher" delivers the message to "the group."

Yet if we look at the human dynamics of the New Testament—who is talking to whom and how people connected—it was very much along peer lines. For example, guild members who had trades (such as Paul's trade as a maker of tents and leather goods) talking to other guild members. Synagogues were hardly the churchlike gathering places we construct in our suburbs today. They were neighborhood meeting places. They were locales where peers met to discuss and learn. How often was Paul invited to talk at a synagogue precisely because he was a guest? (See Acts 13:13–16.)

We see Paul meeting Lydia, to take another example, at a location where people regularly discussed religious and philosophical items of interest. Through this peer exchange Lydia gets interested in Paul's message. In fact, she virtually dares Paul: "If you think I have accepted your word, then come stay in my household" (Acts 16:13–15).

We remember Paul's concerns about what the neighbors of the early Christians would think when they saw their behavior. For example, he tells the Corinthians, "If you say a blessing with the spirit, how can anyone in the position of an outsider say the 'Amen' to your thanksgiving, since the outsider does not know what you are saying?" (1 Cor 14:16). In other words, speak plainly so that others can understand you. By one's peer relationships with others one has an impact on others. Through these give-and-take relationships, faith can begin to be spread.

When we think evangelization, then, it's a good idea to "think peers" because that will yield for us the most fruitful kind of soil in which to sow the seeds of faith. Our neighbors, friends, coworkers and associates are the ones most likely to see our lives and be open to our invitations.

None of this means that we should give up on reaching out to our family members. Aspects and opportunities of faith in the family will come up later. It means that this prior and basic concern for our family members should not distract us from truly fertile fields all around us.

## THE WHAT AND THE HOW

One of the great obstacles to evangelizing activity is the tremendous effort that Catholics have put into *defining* it. Why is this an obstacle? Just consider how many evangelization teams spend years reviewing primary documents about evangelization, only to put off engaging in evangelizing activity until yet more documents are studied?

Obviously our reluctance to evangelize, our fear of actually getting into action, lies behind some of this never-ending need to revisit the *definition* of evangelization. Yet once we get beyond this hesitancy, nothing elates an evangelizing heart more than actually trying to reach others in the name of Christ. A quick look at the "what" and the "how" of evangelization will serve to help us grapple with the idea of Catholic evangelization. And then we can move ahead.

Our Catholic notions of evangelization are very broad. This perhaps is why many keep needing to revisit the definition: they want to take this broad notion and shape it to one or another particular use. The breadth of our Catholic view of evangelization unfortunately does not protect us from people of different ideologies trying to co-opt the word for their own use. This, on top of our instinctual Catholic hesitation about the word *evangelization* in the first place, can make for much inertia.

Yet from the very name of our Church—*Catholic*—we should not be surprised about the breadth of our Catholic understanding of evangelization. That is an asset. We are a worldwide communion that seeks to bring the Gospel to everyone. We believe that God proclaims love in such a way that many different kinds of people can actually hear it. We believe that God encounters us in Jesus and that we are, therefore, called to encounter each other, human-to-human, with the power of the Gospel.

This means that the Word must be spoken in ways that all people can hear, with all their diversity, all their hopes and limitations, all their different life-situations and philosophies. Jesus, coming to his own culture and speaking among his own people, had to keep from being trapped. "Let us head off to other towns," he says, "so that we may proclaim the Good News to all" (Lk 4:43).

## Basic Notion of Evangelization

Although *evangelization* has clusters of meaning besides just a simple notion, Pope Paul VI did, reluctantly, give *evangelization* a definition. In his groundbreaking Apostolic

Exhortation that followed upon the Fourth Synod of Bishops meeting in Rome in 1974, in section 18 of *On Evangelization in the Modern World,* he settles for a definition that, quite quickly, he starts to expand and broaden in the subsequent sections of this exhortation (particularly # 22).

When the U.S. bishops issued *Go and Make Disciples,* they did no more than paraphrase Pope Paul VI. They wrote:

> Evangelizing means bringing the Good News of Jesus into every human situation and seeking to convert individuals and society by the divine power of the Gospel itself. Its essence is the proclamation of the Good News and the response of a person in faith, both being the work of the Holy Spirit.

We can emphasize certain elements of Catholic evangelization from the first part of this definition:

1. It is about the Kingdom of God coming to our human reality in all its fullness; nothing is to be outside the realm of the Kingdom of God.

2. It speaks to individuals, seeking to convert them to the perspective of God.

3. It speaks to societies and cultures, seeking to convert them in their very cultural basis to the perspective of God.

4. It springs from God's Word alone. Force, manipulation, proselytism and exploitive action have no place in evangelization.

Most strikingly, evangelization is never an over-and-done-with matter. Evangelization is not limited to "those who have no God," but rather calls everyone—believer and unbeliever—to conversion and reconversion in spiritual growth and discovery. In this way, our notions of mission, which revolve so much around foreigners and "pagans," have to make room for a broader notion of evangelization that challenges every person to growth in the power of God's Word.

## The "How" of Evangelization

The second part of the U.S. bishops' definition touches on some of its dynamic elements: "Its essence is the proclamation of faith...and the response of a person in faith, both being the work of the Holy Spirit." Proclamation and response, call and answer. This speaks to the human, dialogic, encounter-based dimension that has to accompany evangelization.

We might pause for a moment to appreciate the different ways a "call" has happened in our own lives. Because, simplistically, we can be tempted to translate this idea of "call" into something like walking up and down the street with signs announcing the end of the world. Certainly enough Christians have made such an interpretation and, as a result, have earned the dismissal of their audience.

How has "call" happened to us? What are the ways faith came to us? And kept coming to us? What were the moments in our own lives when we knew we had to grow, to move forward and onward? What are the ways we have continued to respond to the challenge of God's Word?

While we will reflect on these kinds of questions in the next section of this manual, we should, at this point, resist applying naive notions to the way evangelization happens. Indeed, these very naive notions have distorted the way modern people look at evangelization, dismissing it as some kind of honky-tonk marketing strategy or some kind of soupy personal buttonholing of others.

Evangelization occurs in a human dynamic, a call-and-response pattern, that is a form of personal interchange. And it also occurs in the human dynamic of a community, even a church, being challenged by God's Word to respond and grow. Even when, in our heart of hearts, we are grappling with the Word of God deep inside us, this still happens in a context of external behavior, human dynamics and community involvement.

Further, this also says something else about the "how" of evangelization, namely, that it involves reaching out and invitation. The "call" part of evangelization means more than passive sitting or inertia. Most Catholics will readily see themselves, if they practice their faith in any regular way, as *witnesses* to the Gospel. They will point out the pious or devout points of their lives, their efforts at helping others, how they strive to keep the commandments, the quiet way they live their faith. They may even speak with pride about the efforts of Catholic institutions like schools, hospitals, clinics and social resources as great witnesses to the Gospel. And they are. In no way should we Catholics look down on the tremendous efforts we put into *witnessing* to our faith and proclaiming the Gospel in action.

But evangelization also means *proclamation*—invitation and call, above and beyond *witness.* We spread the Gospel by our actions, to be sure, but also by the ways we speak to others about faith and help make it a possibility for them. And as has been noted again and again, we Catholics are entirely too reluctant in this area. As the U.S. bishops put it in *Go and Make Disciples:* "Here, there are two elements at work: *witness,* which is the simple living of the faith; and *sharing,* which is spreading the Good News of Jesus in an explicit way." The bishops say they are eager "to make Catholics in the United States, individually and as a Church, better sharers of God's Good News."

Make no mistake about it: evangelization without witness is hypocrisy. But evangelization that is just witness misses that part of evangelization that involves the universal call to all of God's sons and daughters, to all people, in fact, to all creation.

Of course there are silly, ineffective and manipulative ways to share faith. And there are effective, natural and respectful ways to share faith. Now that we have looked at these basic preliminaries to evangelization, we can, in the next parts of this manual, talk about effective ways of sharing faith first as individuals and, second, in some outreach strategies that parish communities can employ.

# Chapter 2

---

# PERSONAL EVANGELIZATION

Dr. Susan Blum Gerding, director of Isaiah Ministries and a great leader in the evangelization movement in the United States, has long talked about the noninstitutional side of evangelization, which is, actually, the more important side of evangelization—personal evangelization, one-to-one sharing of faith. Church documents freely acknowledge this importance. But they rarely elaborate the many aspects of personal evangelization precisely because there are so many variables, so many particular circumstances and so many individual personalities. These variables and multiple circumstances form richness behind the spreading of faith.

Despite this relative silence, Catholics have to plainly acknowledge the fact that every part of the evangelization effort ultimately comes down to this sooner or later: *individually talking to another person about faith.*

As Pope Paul VI put it so tersely: "In the long run, is there any other way of handing on the Gospel than by transmitting to another person one's personal experience of faith?" (*On Evangelization in the Modern World,* #46).

Despite all the many variations in one-to-one evangelization, however, important things can be said about it. To paraphrase St. Paul's great words on love in the twelfth chapter of his first letter to the Corinthians: "We may erect billboards on every road and even fly messages through the sky, but if we do not talk about faith, heart-to-heart, human-to-human, then we have not evangelization. We may write with the cogency of philosophers and think with the agility of lawyers, but if we have not the ability to share faith in true love with those who are searching, then there is no evangelization."

As we have seen, one-to-one evangelization does not happen in isolation. Whenever any one Catholic Christian talks to another person, he or she brings the eucharistic community, the parish, the Church, along. One-to-one evangelization does not mean "on-my-own" evangelization. After all, if God uses me to touch another, God wants to lead that other person further in faith—to God's Word and to Christ's table, whenever that other person is ready.

So the *process* of one-to-one evangelization begins at the Lord's table and returns to the Lord's table. From that table Catholics, as disciples and bearers of Good News, go forth to bring their faith to the world in love, peace and justice. To that table, in turn, they bring all that God has led them to touch, the cares of the world, and those they meet who also seek a relationship with God in Jesus Christ. As the table fills their hunger, so they are empowered to bring others to have their hunger satisfied.

For this to happen, Catholics need to be prepared in two important ways: (1) they will need to become articulate in their own personal faith, and (2) they will also have to be articulate in the faith of the Catholic people. Once we have looked at these two areas, we can then concentrate on some typical occasions for sharing faith in personal life.

# PERSONAL FAITH

We all hate it when someone tells us what we are feeling.

When, for example, we feel ignored and dismissed but someone tells us that "you are just bored" or "you are imagining something," it only reinforces the first impression we had—that we are not being taken seriously.

Likewise, if we have experienced tremendous loss and someone puts a hand on our shoulder and says, "Don't worry, cheer up, everything will be fine!" our sense of depression only deepens.

Our experience is our experience, we say. Who is to tell us what we are feeling or to advise us to completely ignore these feelings? Experience is basic.

In evangelization, this also is true.

People pay more attention to our experience as human beings than to the large explanations or theories we might propose. Pope John Paul II, in his encyclical on the missions (*Mission of the Redeemer* # 42) offered this smart observation: "People today put more trust in witness than in teachers, in experience than in teaching, and in life and action than in theories." So the most powerful tool we have for evangelization is our own experience as Catholics, an experience by and large unappreciated since we so rarely talk about our experiences of faith to others, even to other Catholics.

Endless speculation about why this is the case should not hide the fact that this relative silence about our personal experience of faith as Catholics can be ended. We *can* learn how to speak. We *can* begin to speak.

After all, when someone tells us about his or her life, do not our ears pick up? As we begin to get a sense of someone's story of how God entered, touched, changed and loved that person, we hang on every point. The faith story has detail in it, incidents that begin to shine and enlighten, persons who played crucial roles, dramatic moments that moved from one seemingly inevitable alternative to another unexpected turn "in the nick of time." We are fascinated by these stories of faith.

Even more, we find them utterly compelling.

Even though our own individual experience might be very different from another's, we give that person every benefit of the doubt because when people speak from the heart, others listen. A friend tells us about powerful encounters after the death of someone he loved—we listen. A coworker tells us about struggles with doubt and shame—we feel right along with her. A neighbor speaks of changes that happened when they started back to church—we cannot ignore it.

Even if, at times, we cannot quite stretch into the experience of others, we take them at their word because they are speaking from the heart. And the heart makes their words compelling and undeniable.

## Not Ignoring Our Own Experience

If this is how it is with others when we hear their experiences, why should it be different with ourselves? When others hear us speaking from our experience, why do we think this will not be a very compelling message for them, even if they never come to believe as we do?

Simple human contact with others has its own powerful witness. Recall, again, the scenes in the Scriptures when Jesus sends his disciples forth to prepare for his upcoming visit. All these visiting incidents take place in Galilee, the home area of Jesus and his disciples. Even so, there was no automatic guarantee of acceptance or success; after all, Jesus warns them about visiting those who do not return a greeting of peace. (See, for example, Lk 10: 6 and 10:10–11.)

Yet the very appearance of two visitors at the door, their very presence, must have brought powerful testimony. After all, when someone stands right in front of you, you must decide something, even if that is only whether to smile or not.

Human presence, and human experience, have a power to announce and verify what no amount of words can quite get across. Even God comes to us in the person of Jesus, right into our human experience.

This power of experience is available to every Catholic who can accept his or her own life of faith. Every one of us can be a witness to what God has done in our lives. To be able to speak that witness, in our own words, in true encounter and with respect for others when they are searching, opens up for us an indispensable resource for helping others discover God.

So the issue in one-to-one evangelization comes down to this: can we Catholics understand and grasp our personal stories of faith? Because once we do, we will be much closer to having the capacity to share faith.

### Finding Our Story

Think about it: each one of us has a personal story of faith. That story may not involve extremely unusual occurrences—how few among us experience ecstasy or direct divine revelation the way St. Paul or St. Francis did? Yet every one of us who believes experiences God and, even more, has experienced the guidance of God in our personal lives.

When did God first plant the seed of faith in our lives? Was it almost from our birth, so that our faith came as a special heritage from our family and parents? Was it during some time of adolescent questioning and growth, so that our faith emerged as part of our human maturing? Maybe our faith was awakened when we went away to college, in the midst of critical challenges, even opposition, or maybe through the many invitations to faith that came through campus ministry. Perhaps our faith lay dormant for a long time, just part of the "furniture" of our lives, until we met a believer with whom we fell in love?

If we reflect on it, we probably can understand our life story as successive stages of faith, with some pivotal moments and long periods of growth and testing. One young man, thinking he had no story of faith, began reflecting on the shift he underwent from attending a small, sheltering parochial grade school to a large public high school. When asked how faith played a role in this rather significant shift, he began to see God's guiding hand and the strength of his faith in ways he had not seen before. Even an "ordinary" life transition like this revealed the hidden hand of God.

Have any of us lived Christian and Catholic lives without undergoing change—change for the better? We might try to identify some of the larger changes in our lives simply to take note of what kind of faith was involved in these. Did we grow closer to Christ? Did we become more like Christ's disciples through these changes? Perhaps we were finally able to put aside a narrow self-centeredness. Or an addiction. Or empty illusions about ourselves. Or careers that led to spiritual dead ends.

Or maybe we turned to something that has become central to our lives, like some spiritual discipline or regular pattern of prayer, or the quiet attendance on the stirrings of the Holy Spirit, or an activity of service to others whose fortune seemed less than ours, or even to renewed relationships with family members.

Every one of these instances is an example of the seedbed of a faith story. Another way of talking about all of this is through the word *conversion.* If we unpack these changes and these patterns in our lives, we will find that they have been instances of growing into Christ Jesus and reaccepting our identity as his followers. The word *conversion* can be used just as much to describe these ordinary life patterns of change as to describe some newfound or life-shattering experience.

These patterns, these changes, these values and these stories are exactly what we have to rediscover about ourselves and share as Catholics with others.

When we start to realize that we each have stories of faith, then the power we have in one-to-one evangelization will become clear to us.

## Important Starting Questions

We might, as an exercise, start asking ourselves some questions and noting our responses. Putting these responses into words opens up for us the outline of the story of our faith, a story that no one can deny or take away from us and, more pointedly, a story that others may find leads them on the road to Christ and returns them to Christ's Church. Here are some important starting questions for our reflection:

- When did faith first come to me?
- Who were the ones who brought it?
- When did I first acknowledge the reality of God?
- What are the most powerful religious moments of my life?
- What changes have I undergone and what role has faith played in them?
- What role have others played in those changes?
- How have I come to think of God? What images, what scriptural stories or sayings speak most deeply to me?
- What are my hopes?
- How does God address my fears? My longings?
- How does God underlie my life values?
- How have I as a believer touched another's faith life?

Reflecting on these and other similar questions can begin to open up our own powerful religious experience, our own story of faith. When we start to get this story down, the next time someone asks, "Why are you Catholic?" we'll be less likely to stare at them speechlessly—and more likely to give "an account of the hope that is within us," as St. Peter suggests (1 Pt 3:15).

*[For a thorough treatment of personal faith stories and a journal workbook to help Catholics discover their stories, see* Discovering My Experience of God: Awareness and Witness, *Kenneth Boyack and Frank DeSiano (Paulist, 1992).]*

## Are You Saved?

Every now and then someone asks a Catholic, "Have you accepted Jesus as your personal Lord and Savior? Are you saved?" Hearing the question, the Catholic is usually baffled, not knowing exactly how to answer.

Such bafflement, however, reflects more a question of style then substance.

For many evangelical and Pentecostal Christians, being a Christian means having a specific, identifiable experience of Jesus, a conversion experience, which culminates in acknowledging Jesus as personal Lord and Savior. Such an experience becomes, for them, a test for Christian reality.

Catholics, many of whom have been raised in the faith from their birth, survey their own life histories in vain; they do not often find a particular experience that matches this kind of "test" for "true Christianity." But this failure should hardly lead Catholics to discount the profound and frequent experiences of God in Jesus through the Spirit that are part of our everyday Catholic life. It should hardly lead them to think the Savior has passed them by and they have no story of faith.

Christianity has developed many "styles" in its history, reflecting many different cultures and many different turns of the human heart. We can see these differences in the wide range of our own personal religious experience. Sometimes we are quiet and contemplative, sometimes we are just faithfully "hanging in," sometimes we are flush with enthusiasm, sometimes we experience such consolations from God that we quake with emotion. Every great mystic has noted phases in Christian life, with the "affective" or "emotive" phase as only one phase, and not the most important phase by a long shot.

When people inquire of Catholics, "Have you accepted Jesus as your personal Lord and Savior?" they are speaking from a particular spiritual tradition with its own style and vocabulary. Catholics, when posed this question, should confidently unpack it and acknowledge that, although we do not use this formula as a regular part of our Catholic expression, everything about our faith speaks to our personal identity with Jesus Christ, his death and resurrection, in loving openness to the will of the Father through the Holy Spirit. We don't talk about "being saved," but about "dying and rising with Christ," a phrase that goes right back to St. Paul. (See Rom 6:3 ff.)

We Catholics should rejoice in the substance of our faith, perhaps no more powerfully revealed than in the reception of holy communion when we are, in faith, united with the very person of Jesus Christ, giving ourselves to him in obedient love and receiving the sacred food that produces the sweetest closeness, short of heaven, we can have with God. This sacred food, by the way, also unites us intimately with every other person in union with Christ.

Our Catholic "style," more liturgical, more contemplative and more communal, is, for all that, not any less an expression of Christian life. Indeed, without these Catholic dimensions, is not Christian life itself truncated? Rather than cringe when questioned, we should feel proud of the breadth of our Catholic heritage.

Being comfortable with our personal stories requires that we look beyond the "styles" of any spiritual expression to the substance of what God has done, and continues to do, in us, giving us the universal vocabulary of human experience, our own faith story, to proclaim the presence of Christ in our lives.

## MY CHURCH'S FAITH

Along with an ability to articulate our own personal faith, Catholics need to have some grasp of the faith of the Church, of the faith story of the Catholic people. As with personal stories of faith, the Church's story of faith seems to present difficulties to Catholics—difficulties that, when examined, may well be exaggerated. As in most Catholic evangelization, deficits always appear larger than assets.

There is a lot of conversation today about "Catholic illiteracy," the widespread post-Baltimore Catechism perception that Catholics, particularly younger ones, cannot articulate the core of their faith, let alone particular distinguishing marks of Catholic faith and life. Compared to the days when Catholics all had "Baltimore Three" down pat, one can certainly argue that Catholics are illiterate about their faith. Even when young men go into the seminary today to study for the priesthood, it is becoming commonplace to offer them an initial period in which to familiarize themselves with "things Catholic," things that were, in the past, the common stock of every altar server.

Granting all of that, the question still remains: how illiterate are Catholics? More pointedly, how literate do Catholics have to be? Must we all be theologians? Must we all have mastered the whole of Scripture, with all the scholarly intricacies? Should the whole storeroom of Catholic history, all twenty centuries of twists and turns, be stored and available in the memory of every Catholic? Must we, in order to articulate our faith, carry an advanced degrees in theology?

## Do We Know Enough?

Once a group of parishioners were being prepared through training for home visiting. As the training ended, the D.R.E. of this particular parish entered the room (she had not been part of the training) and asked how these parishioners could possibly do home visiting if they were not prepared to answer questions about purgatory, Mary, indulgences or other particular Catholic doctrines. Naturally, this concern on the part of the D.R.E. totally undermined the confidence of the would-be home visitors. As a result, the group decided to add an extra session of training, one in which anyone could raise any question to the group, just to see how the visitors might respond.

They were invited to spend the week thinking up particularly difficult questions.

What was the result? All persons in that group, each in his or her own language, responded to the proposed questions from their basic familiarity with the faith and their common sense. They related each "problem" to a part of their Catholic experience and heritage that they had personalized. Mary was a mother and guide; purgatory was our ongoing care for the dead with whom we are joined in Christ; fasting was community discipline; statues were ways of honoring people in our family, just like photos in our homes. The intimidated group discovered that they did, in fact, know their faith and could speak about aspects of it with confidence.

Aside from the fact that these kinds of questions are hardly ever raised when doing home-visiting ministry, the exercise proved that many Catholics, when trusted to express their belief in their own words, can rise to the occasion quite well. True, when Catholics are made to feel scrutinized for exact answers in some kind of contemporary Inquisition, they do clam up and withdraw, because the challenge seems to be asking for something beyond their own familiarity with the Church and its life. They cringe: "What exactly are you asking?" After all, is it not true that anyone can be made to look wrong about this or that aspect of the faith? So with this kind of pressure, Catholics keep quiet. But when Catholics are freed from these kinds of constraints, much of their illiteracy seems to go away.

Knowing the Church's story of faith with a sufficiency to talk to others does not consist in getting degrees in theology or history. It is knowing the central core of the faith and its relevance to the human situation. Beyond this, equipping Catholics with the knowledge of how to find answers to occasional questions that arise (and a particular question might stump the most learned of us) should give them the confidence to feel that they can articulate the Church's story of faith.

Our contemporary fashion is to doubt ourselves. We know all too well how to make ourselves look inadequate. However, we Catholics might trust a bit more what happens every Sunday, what happens in daily life, what happens in scores of thousands of small groups that share faith and personal support, what happens even through reading religious newspapers and magazines: the faith gets passed on and deepened.

## Core of Faith

Knowing the core of the Catholic faith and its relevance to the human situation will equip Catholics with a basic framework for both understanding and articulating the faith. This core can be reinforced by ready reference to *The Catechism of the Church, The Catholic Encyclopedia* or other standard Catholic catechetical reference books. Priests, religious and laypersons who have advanced degrees in theology are readily available to Catholics in their parishes or campus ministries. Most dioceses also have Catholic information centers that can provide an approach to answer a particular question. In other words, Catholics have skills and resources.

What are the key elements in the core of Catholic faith with which Catholics should be familiar? This brief table, developed from the elements of the Creed that Catholics recite every Sunday, might serve as a helpful reminder. The credal statements are coordinated with various ways to relate them to human concerns and also with references to *The Catechism of the Church* (CC).

| CREDAL STATEMENT | ASPECTS OF HUMAN RELEVANCE |
|---|---|
| We believe in one God, creator of all (CC #295-301) | Every human heart searches for absolutes, every human seeks to know the "why" of his or her life. |
| Who has sought to gather all humankind in love (CC # 759-769) | Whatever our differences, we know we are called to love each other and live together as one. This love reflects God's universal love in our lives. |
| Who has been revealed in every age and era (CC #50-55) | The signs of God are present everywhere; virtually every society has developed some faith in a supreme transcendent being. |
| But most especially in the experience of Israel, which we find in the Jewish Scriptures (the Old Testament) (CC # 56-64) | To read the Scriptures is to be filled with faith, inspiration and direction; also, it is to be called into relationship with God. They enlighten all who read them. |
| We believe in Jesus Christ, God's only Son, who was born a member of the Jewish people from a virgin (CC #430-507) | Jesus uniquely embodies this personal relationship with God, drawing on the depth of the Jewish Scriptures to reveal God as "Father" and calling people to love God totally and love others as themselves. Mary has a unique relationship to Jesus because of her discipleship as his mother, a relationship recognized throughout the Scriptures. |
| This Jesus gathers all people into a new experience of God (CC #238-48; 422-51; 2558-65; 2598-2616) | Jesus, appearing in the human flesh, touches all human flesh and relates to all human history and experience. In his person, he relates all humans to God through his divinity. |

| Through his preaching, life, death and resurrection (CC #535–655) | Jesus speaks to the very force of sin and death in our lives through his own death and resurrection, which open up a new dimension of hope and life for people. This makes Jesus unique in human and religious history. Every human, no matter how strong the denial, must deal with the mystery of death. |
|---|---|
| We believe in the Holy Spirit (CC # 683–741) | The God we believe in is not just creator and savior; God is also intimately within us as lover, consoler and inner power. God also continues the saving work of Jesus through the Spirit's presence in the world. |
| Who gathers us into a Church that is one, holy, catholic and apostolic (CC #763–801) | The quest for unity among people begins its effective realization in the people Christ forms through the Spirit. This people is a prophetic herald of the human unity of which we dream. |
| A Church God has endowed with the gifts to authentically proclaim the Gospel (CC # 849–65) | God's gift of the Spirit keeps Christ's community faithful to the Good News of salvation; this fidelity is guarded by the leaders and the whole people of the Church. The human heart longs to know the truth and be secure in it. |
| A community of people who share the Scriptures and the sacred sacraments (CC #1345–1405) | Our need for wisdom and our need for holiness are shaped by the Easter gifts of the Holy Scriptures and the sacraments, which unite us with Christ and each other and make us Christ's Church. |
| The sacraments initiate us; they also equip us for Christian life | Baptism joins us to Christ, a unity that is intensely and intimately |

| and service (CC #1212-1314; 1536-89; 1601-58) | brought about in our eucharistic worship and the holy communion with the person of Jesus. Confirmation concludes the process of initiation with the gift of the fullness of the Holy Spirit. Marriage and priesthood are ways that our baptismal calls are shaped to specific lives of service. |
|---|---|
| And because we believe in the forgiveness of sin, we celebrate the sacraments of forgiveness and healing (CC #1442-70; 1500-25) | Reconciliation brings us the peace we need when we have broken our relationships with God and others; it celebrates the forgiveness at the heart of all Christian life. Anointing shows God's healing of the human body and spirit. The capacity for new life, for starting over, for healing and pardon is never exhausted. |
| We believe in the communion of saints—the place of Mary and the saints, prayer for the deceased, communal holiness (CC #946-72) | None of us lives alone, but in union with others; this union extends to those who have gone before us and now live in God. The saints are our brothers and sisters in faith. Christ's community transcends death. |
| We believe that we will rise again and enjoy unending life—life beyond death, heaven, hell and purgatory (CC #992-1014) | The quest for immortality that lies behind so many cultures and surfaces in every human heart is attained in the salvation that Jesus won for us. Heaven, hell and purgatory speak of the states of life we attain after death. Salvation or damnation, the fruit of final judgment, represent the ultimate choices for us and mirror our lifelong choices of good or evil. |

One can elaborate this short schema of the story of the Church's faith in endless ways because the Gospel has been reflected on and experienced for two thousand years. However much we elaborate on the Gospel and show its complexities, this is not as important as the clear outline of the Church's teaching, the "kergyma," the proclamation of Good News that people long to hear and, really, need to hear. Every practicing Catholic basically knows this kerygma of Good News, if only as a seed.

But how does this Good News get spread? How might modern people come to that hearing? In what ways might we Catholics have opportunities for one-to-one evangelization? One part of that answer lies in the personal sharing of faith.

## PERSONAL OCCASIONS FOR FAITH SHARING

Equipped with a grasp of our own faith story and with a sense of the marvelous story of faith that our Church constantly tells, we Catholics need not avoid the many situations in which opportunities are given to witness, share and invite.

Often, however, many of these opportunities go unrecognized. People drop huge hints and, like a prepubescent teenager when it comes to romance, we don't have a clue what those hints might mean. We often react protectively or defensively, moving more deeply into ourselves when we could otherwise be engaging another person, face-to-face, in encounter and dialogue.

### Proselytism and Manipulation

Catholics crawl into their protective shells because instinctively they reject proselytism and religious manipulation, those unfair and disrespectful tactics that sometimes are used to undermine another's faith. Having been victimized often by these kinds of tactics, Catholics can come to feel that any sharing of faith, any religious dialogue, might come across as some kind of religious trickery or arm-twisting.

If we truly encounter another, with respect and tact, seeking to meet and love that other person more deeply in Christ, there should be no danger of the proselytism, manipulation or insensitive badgering that characterize some of the actions that have given evangelism a bad name. Evangelization is not evangelism, in the sense that evangelism often in modern society looks like a form of religious aggression. The human context in which people honestly meet people and let them keep their full freedom always forms the framework for evangelization. The horizon of the Kingdom of God, in its breadth and compassion, always attends the work of evangelization. This is all the truer when people approach us, directly or indirectly, about our faith.

So we modern Catholics, faced with many opportunities for sharing faith, need not wither away. We can dialogue and share as comfortably as Jesus did with tax collectors, Martha and Mary, and others like the Samaritan woman, with love and respect for the freedom of the human heart. These kinds of opportunities abound in modern life. What might some of these approaches look like?

### *Example #1: Facing Charlie the Critic*

Every time the newspaper carries a story about the pope or some bishop, it seems Charlie has a comment, usually a biting comment or even an outright negative one. "Pope this, pope that, who cares?" he might grunt as he looks at his newspaper. Or, "I guess people who cannot think for themselves need someone to help them know what to think." These kinds of comments might be said offhandedly or belligerently before a group of fellow workers, or even to a particular Catholic, by the watercooler or over a salad at lunch. Charlie thinks he's on the hunt.

Before we let Charlie drive us crazy, it might be good to ask ourselves, "Why does Charlie make the comments that he makes?" Most people do not talk this way, so why does Charlie? He seems negative, but what is he really up to?

It could possibly be that Charlie is searching. Perhaps Charlie is just curious, or just afraid of his own religious insecurity. So he plays the game of getting a "rise" out of someone whom he really might like to share with. Of course, Charlie could just be a mean person, harping and biting, a kind of bully. In that case, our own antennae will tell us not to engage Charlie except to limit the damage of his intemperate remarks and show the basic compassion of Christ.

However, if Charlie really is asking us questions, is probing and testing, why be shy? After all, he opened up the issue. We can respond to Charlie in such a way that we find out whether being a critic is all he wants to be—or whether he is a searcher too. After all, the pope has become the most important religious figure in our news; the pope stimulates people, by his ministry, to think about themselves and the meaning of their lives. Millions of people who are not Catholic are positively affected by his visits and his words. The pope is "public material." Should these opportunities be lost?

One can test Charlie's heart by simply addressing his question, stripping it of any snideness. If Charlie says something in a group, one can reply to Charlie in the group, "Well, the role of the pope is very complicated and very important. I'd love to tell you what the pope has meant in my own life."

If Charlie is whispering to us by the watercooler, we can just look Charlie in the face and say, "Charlie, you know I'm a Catholic, right? If you want to talk to me about the pope, I'd really love to chat with you. Can we do this after work today? Maybe I can clear up some misimpressions."

Beginning with the pope (or any other religious item that Charlie might have tossed about), we have the opportunity to open up the range of our personal experience and appreciation of the faith. We can confront Charlie's seeming hostility with a compassionate Catholic face that he has to respect. Who knows, Charlie might find a much better answer than he ever suspected! Charlie might even find faith.

People who criticize a lot are sometimes very curious. If there is any openness, our openness to them in turn can provide them approaches on a level deeper than their barbs.

## Example #2: Calming Annie the Anxious

We see Annie every now and then. Whenever we run into her, she's wringing her hands and in a tizzy. Annie is anxious about everything. Her life might, in fact, be fairly serene and stable, but Annie never seems to realize that. She expresses fears for her husband, her children, whether she is doing the right thing, whether she should decide this way or that way about an issue, fears about everything. She doesn't seem able to even prepare for her weekly shopping, so anxious is she that something might be overlooked or forgotten.

What is the source of Annie's anxiety? Why does everything become a potential crisis or some major issue? Whatever her gifts, whatever her resources—and she has them—they never seem enough.

What is missing in Annie's life, of course, is the fruit of faith: trust. She will be anxious so long as she believes that wringing her hands and dripping stomach acid actually solves something or makes her world better. The prospect of leaving things in God's hands and wringing her own a little less has not dawned on Annie because, way down deep, it seems like it's all up to her.

When Annie expresses her anxiety to us, shows us her hysterical side that cannot be calmed, isn't that an opportunity for sharing faith? Although we cannot dismiss Annie's feelings, and while we recognize that her anxiety may be tied to deep elements in her personality, her anxiety still is an opportunity to show the trust and peace that has come to us through faith.

To Annie's anxiety, we can simply start by rejoining, "I know what it's like to worry all the time, but I've found that it's a waste of time. I've found something that works better for me." We can narrate an anxious time in our lives and how we found our worry to be a good bit of useless energy. We can express what happens when, in prayer, we place our worries in the hands of God. We can even invite Annie to join us in this kind of prayer. We can point out in the Scriptures how Jesus teaches us the uselessness of worry (Mt 6:31 ff.) or pray a psalm that brings great comfort (e.g., Ps 23).

Annie's anxiety invites us to share the fruits of our faith. It is an opportunity to bring the Gospel.

### Example #3: Freeing Sally the Sad

Sally has every reason to be sad, having helped her husband through some very difficult times, which arose from a long-standing illness. In spite of all her efforts, her husband died and she feels alone, bereft, bereaved.

She keeps her husband's picture in many of the rooms of her house. She seems incapable, after an appropriate period of time, of packing up and appropriately disposing of his possessions. His possessions are arranged like a shrine. She frequently makes her husband the main topic of her conversation with her children and her friends, even with passing strangers.

Sally says she believes in God and, like most people in our society, believes in an "afterlife." She prays with some regularity but finds it hard to pray deeply because it reminds her of her deceased husband. She's been to bereavement groups and says that they help. But she cannot let go, and the process of clutching onto her husband's memory makes it impossible for her to go on with her life. "I can't believe that he died like that and left me alone," she complains. We can almost physically register her pain.

What Sally has not experienced, however, is the faith that comes from the resurrected Christ. She has not been able to make the "paschal mystery," the mystery of death and resurrection, into an active part of her attitude toward life. She's kept religion to a certain sincere, but limited, sphere in her life. So her grief has come to occupy the gap that her limited faith has left.

When Sally expresses her grief, she gives us the opportunity to proclaim the heart of our Christian faith, the power of Christ Jesus over death through his risen life. No dimension of our faith speaks more clearly to the human situation than the death and resurrection of Jesus Christ. Of course, her grief might come from a variety of places, even from deeply unfulfilled parts of her life that her husband's death only reinforced. Her grief might be a sign of sickness. But our ability to listen to people like Annie in their grief and anxiety—our ability to encounter people in their sorrow—remains an indispensable key to opening the door to our sharing with them and helping them begin to absorb our faith.

Our experience of faith and hope, even in the face of death, can begin to open Sally to other ways to understand her life and her husband's death. Her inability to stop the feeling that she's been cheated by death arises from the broadly felt human sentiment that death cuts life short, that we were made for something more than our seventy or eighty years, that our life does point to something transcendent. So Sally's grief gives us an opportunity to share our experience of the risen Christ, to review our own times of grief, to say how we learned to pray "Alleluia" even when our hearts were filled with tears. "God knows our death. God died for us in Christ Jesus just so we'd know how fully God shares our human experience. Christ is risen. I know this. I have found this again and again in the hardest times of my life. Let me tell you about the God that Jesus reveals to us." The freedom Christ's faith has brought to

us might, through a loving interchange, free Annie from a grief
that needlessly cripples her.

### Example #4: Bantering with Competitive Chris

Brash is something of an understatement when it comes to
Chris. He's a true champion, a competitor with life and with
everyone in it. Chris is a winner. From his earliest years he's
had a source of energy and passion that left him, and everyone
around him, totally restless.

Chris had to be "tops." Whether it was spelling, or math, or
Monopoly, Chris had to win. On the playground, Chris's team
always came out ahead and he, of course, was the star. As he
grew up, the need to win, to be successful, to have the 4.0, the
best sporting averages and the "prettiest girl" were Chris's
total obsession.

Now Chris is our coworker and perhaps soon will be our
boss. It isn't that he just rides all over people; it's that he never
stops, never puts things in perspective, never seems to tire,
and always has to win. Every once in a while, perhaps, Chris
seems tired or expresses a doubt. But he buries that doubt in a
fresh spate of "What Makes Sammy Run" energy that covers
over his fatigue.

Hard as it might be to share with Chris, and necessary as it is
for him to hide his insecurity, Chris needs the Gospel. Not
because it's always wrong to want to win, but because it's dis-
astrous not to be at peace with oneself, whether one is winning or losing. Run as Chris might, some day he will run out of
energy, of creativity, of orientation and direction. Chris, after
all, has all the short-term goals clear in his head, but hasn't a
clue about what the long-term goal really is.

Because it's hard to share with Chris, a believer must have a
long-term strategy and especially look for opportunities to
raise long-term questions: Why are we pursuing this? Is winning right at any cost? If we attain this, what will it really mean

in terms of the underlying values of our company, or, more pointedly, the underlying values of life?

Most important, who will be there when Chris starts not to win, when he loses for the first time, or really loses big? From both a positive and a negative side, we might start opening up faith questions for the Chrises of the modern world and, in the process, do them a great service. By doing this, we might make it possible for them to drop their obsessions and to see moral and spiritual issues as more important than the crazy obsession that drives their need to win.

Jesus never put down ambition. Remember his parable of the wise steward who knew how to cut a deal, or the parables of those who received the talents? (See, e.g., Lk 16:1–9 and Mt 25:14–29.) Jesus never put down ambition, but for him it was a metaphor of the true ambitions of life, the integrity of our souls and the pursuit of the Kingdom.

By our friendly question raising and by our willingness to be around for even people who might intimidate us, we make the Kingdom accessible when people are ready to consider it. "What gain does one have if the whole world is possessed, but one's soul is lost?" (See Mk 8:36.)

## Those Around Us

Perhaps we recognize our own versions of Charlie, Sally, Annie or Chris; perhaps these simple vignettes have helped us see the ways that opportunities for faith abound, particularly for those who are comfortable with their own faith and are willing to encounter others in love, hearing them and responding to them in appropriate human ways. The point is this: opportunities abound in daily life for us to share honestly and appropriately from the deep perspective of our faith. These constitute true evangelizing situations. The Spirit begs us not to waste them.

We each could sketch dozens of life situations that call for a response of faith. One-on-one, life provides endless variations on how faith can be evoked. However, there also exist certain thresholds in daily life that provide general settings for sharing faith. It might be helpful to look at some of these kinds of situations where faith can also be shared in an appropriate way.

## THRESHOLDS: DAILY SITUATIONS

The plan and strategy for evangelization issued by the U.S. bishops, *Go and Make Disciples,* sees evangelization taking place in "the home, the workplace and in today's many cultural settings." This phrase deliberately attempts to locate evangelization more outside its "churchy" settings and in the arenas where human sharing and exchange naturally happen. These broader settings form thresholds in which faith can take on an appropriate role, thresholds both for the active Catholic who can bring Good News to others and for those who are questioning, seeking, needing Good News.

Once we become sensitive to the various signals that others might send us about their readiness to dialogue about faith or provide a one-to-one opportunity for sharing faith, the thresholds of daily situations, the general settings of our daily life, also begin to take on faith-filled possibilities.

We can explore some of these in the sections ahead.

## THE WORKPLACE

### *Rules of the Workplace*

Nowhere is sensitivity more demanded than the workplace. Here the classic "separation of church and state" becomes enshrined in the modern "separation of faith and daily life." The workplace is professional, has its own rules of conduct and discourse and has its own purposes—usually, making money, or at least enough money to pay salaries.

The salary system enforces the rules of the workplace. People are employed so they might be paid. If rules are broken or employees are not serving the economic purposes of the workplace, then deprivation of payment through firing is the usual result. Can there be a more powerful motivator for preserving the ethos of the workplace?

Even so, workplaces are not all the same. Some are very formal and others are quite casual. Some have a highly enforced style while others have more the flavor of a large extended family. Some work situations allow very little contact between employees; others are seedbeds of great friendships.

Fundamentally everyone has a right to come to work, accomplish the job and receive compensation without constraint. If religion has a role in the workplace, then respect for this freedom, this absence of constraint, is absolutely necessary. Any of us who have felt "hounded" by a coemployee or even "harassed" by a boss who seemed to demand something from us as part of our work know what a violation this unwarranted constraint is.

As Catholics, with our fundamental belief in the sacredness of conscience and the right everyone has to religious liberty, we know that any form of proselytism, any twisting of arms, any implied quid pro quo in the supposed name of religion, stands as an offense against our belief in the dignity of the human person and the freedom of the Gospel.

With these clear boundary lines in view, however, there are two workplace settings where faith can have appropriate and vital impact: the values we bring to our job and the spaces of privacy that the workplace allows throughout the day. In each of these settings we remain disciples of Christ with the capacity to bring Christ's vision to others. We do this, however, as employees, incarnating in the workplace the dynamics of Christ. In other words, we are not priests, missionaries, fanatics, meddlers or peddlers. We are professional workers who also are disciples.

## Sharing Our Values

Values? Morality? What can be more sectarian, more threat-eningly religious, than that? Aren't values just the things people in our society don't want "shoved down their throats," as it is so often put? We instinctually stay away from issues of morality and sin for fear we will seem like disgruntled prophets trying to throw cold water on everyone else's party.

All of this would be true if values were something "sectar-ian," that is, something that came only from a private group with private views. Of course, there are elements about Catholic life that are sectarian—going to church on Sunday or rules of fasting—that come solely from our internal Church life and discipline. But that is true of only some of our positions.

Apart from these internal and disciplinary matters, many of our deepest values as Catholics spring from the inherent quali-ties of the human person and human society itself. These deep values do not depend on the particular teachings of Catholic life and faith; they rest on what everyone can affirm as essen-tial for human life to exist and to have meaning. They are val-ues that spring from human life itself.

No church has been clearer about these values and rights than has the Catholic Church. In a virtually unbroken chain, Catholics have expressly reflected on the "social values" inher-ent in life for well over a century, prompted by the great changes brought about through the industrial revolution and modern life. We have no reason to flinch in light of this body of thought, based as it is on human good; indeed, we have every reason to turn to it for fresh vision about the meaning of human life—vision for ourselves and vision for the world.

## Do Values Belong in the Workplace?

Do these values belong in the workplace? Of course they do. Do they belong there because the Catholic Church teaches them? No, not because of that, but because they are necessary for the human person and for human society to survive and thrive. Catholic arguments for these values do not rest only on the commandments or on Church teaching; they rest on human reflection, on consideration of what it means to be a just society.

Because these values belong in the workplace, and in every human sector of life, every Catholic has a right to point appropriately to them in the decision making of the company. The word *appropriate* means here that we articulate our views as a voice in the development of the policy of our workplace using the channels that are made available to us. It also means we point to these values using arguments that arise from our inherent human rights rather than arguments that depend solely on religious doctrine. Sometimes it may take years for a company to shift values in one direction rather than another. Far better to be known as a helpful participant—with a chance to continue influencing values—than as a nag or a religious fanatic whose ideas will be dismissed by everyone else.

What are some of the elements of the Church's social teaching? The following list, with references to those elements in *The Catechism of the Catholic Church,* will provide a starting place:

- The importance and the value of the family (CC #2207 ff.)
- The importance of every person, without any exception, because of the value of human nature itself, creating respect, equality and solidarity as basic attitudes among human beings (CC #1929-44)
- The freedom, in family life, to start a family; be protected from instability; profess and live faith; own private property; obtain work and housing; emigrate; receive medical care and other forms of social security; be free from drugs, pornography, alcoholism; associate with other families (CC #2211)

- The right to be educated and to choose a profession or state of life (CC #2223 ff.)
- The duty of citizens to contribute to the good of society and serve their country as well as to resist unjust and immoral laws (CC #2238 ff.)
- The right to receive personal respect and to defend oneself (CC #2263 ff.)
- The right to life (CC #2273)
- Respect for the reputation and health of others (CC #2284 ff.)
- Respect for proper scientific research and the right of people not to be exploited for such purposes (CC #2292 ff.)
- Respect for the integrity of all creation (CC #2415 ff.), and the use of the world's resources for the good of all (CC #2403 ff.)
- The integrity of justice, contracts, promises (CC #2408 ff.)
- The right to seek and obtain employment, to exercise economic initiative, to receive a just wage, to organize, to strike; the responsibilities of the state and business enterprises to foster these values (CC #2426 ff.)
- The place of justice and peace between nations (CC #2437 ff.)
- Respect for truth and professional secrets (CC #2488 ff.)
- The proper use of communications and social media (CC #2493 ff.)

## Expressing Our Values in the Workplace

These human values, based on the inherent needs of human nature, can take on a crucial relevance when they inform the way we think and choose as professionals, as business people, as participants in the workplace. Would we prefer that the decisions by which society is guided derive from a so-called valueless stance or, as is more likely, from corrupted values? As disciples who have proper roles in this workplace, we can bring these positive human values to life by our input into policy and business decisions, thereby bringing the Kingdom of God more clearly into our modern world.

Some examples might help:

- A management team decides about policies in the workplace. A Catholic on the team can emphasize principles of justice, fairness and respect for the person.
- Coworkers start joshing a worker because of prejudices or cultural differences. As a Catholic, one can support the worker and try to mediate with the other workers.
- Partners know that winning a case is important and are willing to bend, or even break, rules to accomplish that. A committed Catholic can give true witness about the importance of integrity and truth beyond the pressure of the immediate case.
- One's teenager runs with a crowd for whom "brand-name labels" are all-important. Giving the teen some possibility of resisting the commercialism can actually reinforce the basic sense of worth that the youth needs to develop wholesomely.
- Associates are attacking newcomers to our country as lazy, unproductive or parasitic immigrants. As a Catholic, one can give witness to one's friends by tactfully calling attention to the difficulties that cause and attend immigration and to the human issues at play in these migratory patterns.
- A coworker at lunch is proposing ideas about abortion or euthanasia that appear to overlook basic values of life. They also contain misinformation. An informed Catholic can inject in a fitting way other ideas that support life's values and provide correct information on these issues.

- A personnel director has called a meeting to look at health and pension benefits to make recommendations to the corporation. When the fundamental values that drive the meeting seem to be "saving the bottom line," other issues of justice, from a Catholic perspective, can be raised as important assets with which the company might wish to identify.
- One has suffered an injury and has received advice to begin a lawsuit. Knowing the potential hurt that a lawsuit might cause others, a believer might choose instead some kind of mediation or arbitration to redress any wrong.
- One discovers that one's firm has engaged in fraud. Standing up for the truth and forcing the company to correct its fraud and make restitution can be a heroic act of human and Christian witness that can benefit many.

### We Can Make a Difference in the Workplace

Catholics are now a powerful presence at every level in society, from the very highest corporate levels to the most essential laborers doing the most menial work. Knowing that the workplace is, in its own right, a field for bringing Good News, Catholics can make a huge difference in the way our society works. We can do this not as righteous "goody-goodies" who make everyone else feel resentful and put down, but as an inner force that transforms society through profound human values. Doing this starts to bring to life the vision of the third goal articulated by the U.S. bishops in *Go and Make Disciples:* fostering Gospel values in our society and working for the importance of the family and the common good. It's well past time for Catholics to step up to the plate in this area.

### Faith in our "Private Spaces" on the Job

Every workplace provides private space, even in the midst of its office or factory environment. Lunch periods, coffee breaks, company outings or parties, time before the "clock" starts or time after work are just some examples of this "private space."

Christians are using these periods to foster faith in their daily lives. Catholics sometimes join other Christians in these efforts at faith development—but they rarely initiate these opportunities themselves. And they can. One parish, for example, rents a dining room downtown for lunch once a month; it invites all its professionals who work in the area to join together in faith and sharing.

Whatever the "ethos" of our work environment, what we do with our free time is up to us. It is *free* time. What opportunities lie in these free moments? Again, we are always bound to act with great courtesy and tact, even if we are free to use our spare time as we want on the workplace. A worker, for example, who uses the coffee break to put holy cards on the desks of coworkers is violating a taboo. It is unlikely that such efforts will be rewarded with success. Likewise, a worker who uses the lunch period to sing hymns in his or her cubicle will probably not gain the admiration of coworkers or bosses.

With these cautions in mind, however, it still remains true that these free periods before, during and after work can be opportunities for appropriate faith sharing.

These might be times, for example, when the worries or fears of a coworker allow us the chance to talk, bringing guidance and consolation. These might be times to invite coworkers with whom one has formed a friendly relationship to one or another event at one's church. Free periods might also allow one to organize workers around an important cause, to help another coworker in trouble, for instance, or to provide help at Christmas for some struggling family. They might even be opportunities for shared prayer or scriptural reflection.

Realizing that forming a relationship with others is an indispensable need for sharing faith, a Catholic begins to evangelize by the way one allows others into his or her personal life even in the workplace. These personal relationships, which network through the workplace (and really make it effective), are workplace opportunities for communicating our values and being comfortable with our faith.

The evangelization team of a parish might spur some very interesting actions by offering open-ended workshops to help parishioners explore workplace spirituality and faithsharing. This team might also spearhead organizing parishioners who work in a downtown area to build faith by witnessing and sharing. Catholics, now in an important position to touch the workplace, will know what is possible and what might be effective. Poised as we are in society, we Catholics should have no trouble imagining all the possibilities.

## HOUSEHOLDS

When the Church speaks of the family as a "miniature church" *(ecclesiola)*, it may strike many Catholics as a bit of hyperbole. "My house?" we think. "Can't be." Not much sacred seems to happen in our Catholic households, does it? How could it be a "miniature church"?

And yet our family lives can be one of the great resources for evangelizing the world, both the little world of our own homes and the larger world that our homes touch—our wider families, friends and neighbors. We might well imagine how difficult it could be for someone to enter or investigate the Catholic Church just by stopping by a church or going to a rectory; how much easier would all that be if people could be touched by Catholic faith through their normal contact with Catholic neighbors?

A story has been told about a relatively active Catholic family who moved into a new neighborhood. Neighbors to one side of the house immediately came over and welcomed them. They were invited to the neighbors' church—a Baptist church. Even though they declined the invitation, a great friendship was struck between the two families, including opportunities for praying together and sharing faith.

The neighbors on the other side of the house never even said "hello," and were almost total strangers until one Sunday morning, when help was needed on this neighbor's car. After names were exchanged and help was given, the near-stranger invited his neighbor to come in for coffee. His neighbor declined because it was almost time for Mass. "You're a Catholic?" the near-stranger asked. "So am I." But the neighbor thought, "Who would ever have known?" The Catholic neighbor had no notion of his house as a "little church."

If faith is spread through friendship and human association, then the family, with all its myriad connecting relationships, can be a powerful field for witnessing to faith and inviting to faith others who are searching.

This presumes, of course, that something *is* going on in our homes in terms of faith. Religious people, who are unfortunately deeply swayed by the lifestyles of today's rat-race world, must resist the tendency to make their homes little more than convenient staging areas for individual activities—getting off to work, doing homework, getting ready for the game, grabbing a bite, taking care of bodily needs, going out to the movies, falling exhausted into bed.

Many modern families hardly *talk* to each other, let alone let that talk be grounded in and flower into prayer and spiritual sharing. Yet we continue to wonder why family life grows colder, why people have a hard time expressing love and finding security, why they feel ever so more isolated from each other.

Catholics have to start reversing this by having regular time and space for prayer, shared prayer, spiritual and scriptural reflection; doing this would, at the same time, foster some kind of human interchange that could provide strength for resisting the dissipating quality of modern life.

And to underline the obvious, families that had spiritual centers would naturally—without any pretense or holier-than-thou smugness—be revealing their core of faith to others. Some ways this aspect of personal evangelization, through the family, can happen are given below as ways to entice our Catholic imaginations toward the many opportunities to share faith through family life.

## A Child Is Born

The birth of a child automatically grips lives, not just the mother's or the father's, and not just the sisters' or brothers' lives—everyone is curious about the birth of a baby.

"How many months?" "It's not twins, is it?" "A boy or a girl, do you know yet?" "Is the pregnancy hard?" "Boy you are big!" "I hope you're not making your wife work too much around the house." "What are you going to name the baby?"

These and dozens of similar phrases are ways that many people get involved when a pregnancy occurs—family members, relatives, friends, acquaintances and even strangers.

The natural curiosity that people have—above and beyond direct statements of faith that parents can make to their friends during the pregnancy—can be more sharply focused when it comes time to baptize the child. Many of our neighbors will not believe in baptism; others will have shrugged baptism off by saying, "I'll let my child choose her faith when she grows up." Others of our friends will believe in baptism but only as a cultural vestige.

So the committed Catholic family has a real opportunity to frame a whole vision of faith for those who gather at the baby's "christening." Their involvement in preparing for baptism, their care in choosing godparents who witness faith, their hospitality to those who come to the church, and their witness around the family celebration can be powerful statements of faith.

A baby is born: dare we say what it means, what God's gift means to those who gather, what Christ's life brings that child and that family, the Christian hopes parents have for their child? Would not this be a perfect time to invite people to join hands around the baby, express their feelings, and participate in prayers that godparents might lead? The Catholic parents can give a far more powerful homily about the meaning of faith and baptism than the celebrating priest. What is more, the guests are more likely to be listening.

A child is born...and Good News can be proclaimed.

## A Parent Dies

Like birth, death grabs people's attention.

Baby boomers, who, along with their children, make up a large portion of "unchurched" people in today's society, all have the difficult task of watching their parents age and die. Though modern culture may deny death in all its forms, the undertaker still gets called when death makes its inevitable visit.

How Catholics view the process of aging, becoming infirm and dying speaks eloquently about our real faith. Every time a neighbor asks about an aging or dying parent, it is an opportunity to reflect faith. Sermons are not needed; the faith that radiates in the life of a believer spontaneously shows itself at these moments.

The evangelized Catholic has ample opportunity in these moments to challenge the "people don't die" or "death doesn't hurt" veneer that gets smeared over everything today. And to counterpoint the "doesn't she look wonderful?" remarks people feel they have to make over the open casket.

Catholics who have faith can use the whole dying process, the wake service, the funeral and the gathering after the funeral to speak of life's meaning and life's hopes beyond death.

In these days, when it's obvious to everyone that the unchurched show up for weddings and funerals, the witness and proclamation that a believing Catholic can give to his neighbors and friends, to her relatives and associates, when death does visit will proclaim the Gospel through a vision of life and hope that modern life so often stifles.

### Catholic Witness at Special Celebrations

As Catholics have been "acculturated" to the broad and bland middle-class attitudes of today's world, their feasts have lost the focus of faith—the faith from which these feasts sprang to begin with.

Christmas—it's Santa Claus. Easter—it's the Bunny. St. Patrick's Day—it's the bottle or Irish jigs. Thanksgiving—it's the start of the shopping season or even, as some call it, "Turkey Day"! Nostalgia is the theme for New Year's, and we rent thriller movies for Halloween night.

How do we celebrate these feasts, particularly those that are overtly religious? What is the tenor of the parties that we throw? Cannot the parties that we throw, the tables that we set, the music we play, the invitations we send—cannot these be statements of faith?

After all, several religious groups make large statements by *refusing* to celebrate these feasts at all, denouncing all feasts as pagan derivatives or something supposedly forbidden in the Scriptures. What would happen if those of us who believe in the religious sense behind these festivals used them as opportunities to reveal faith to our neighbors and friends, or at least to make them more comfortable with the faith behind them?

A Christmas party—certainly a warm retelling of the Christmas story makes sense. Children can even act it out!

Easter dinner—around the table, mentioning those who have died in the past year, the special hope that Easter brings, those who have entered the Church, the signs of divine renewal—all make much more sense than chocolate eggs and white bunnies.

Birthdays, anniversaries and other celebrations of congratulations can all have a faith dimension. Imagine a birthday celebrant thanking God for one more year of life as the candles get blown out.

Again, the more our faith is part of our daily life, the more these events can become evangelizing moments without seeming strained or self-righteous. Jesus went to a lot of dinner parties and gave many parables about kingly parties; he must have known these were great times to reveal the Kingdom.

## Times for Family Faith Sharing

*Renew* and many other parish processes have brought about a new phenomenon in Catholic life—the small faith-sharing group.

The theme of these groups might be the Bible; but it might also be religious themes of a more general type. Most of these groups are for *sharing,* although some are for *study.* Whatever they are, the fact is that hundreds of thousands of Catholics have become involved in these shared moments.

What often happens, however, is that these groups become somewhat "closed," dwindling down to three or four couples who get into a beautiful routine that is still routine nonetheless. Even more worrisome is the often-made observation that once these groups get closed, they have a hard time welcoming new people into the group.

Yet can there be a better forum than faith sharing for inviting others into the group, particularly those who question their faith or who need support through difficult faith transitions? Why cannot the very dynamism of these groups help them to grow, extending welcome to others and, in the process, extending faith to others?

The character of these groups can often lend itself to participation by unchurched people or "inactive" Catholics. Part of the power of these groups is the evangelizing potential that becomes apparent when they are being formed, a potential that often gets spent and exhausted in the early part of the process.

Just as we can be personally shy, reluctant to meet someone new, so also we can be communally shy, reluctant to welcome new people—and *welcome* is the only process by which groups can begin to share faith.

The Catholic household is a potential sharing zone for faith. If the millions of households that claim the name "Catholic" started to mine the evangelizing potential of their home life, started to more clearly live and more freely show their faith, our twenty thousand parishes would be augmented by a huge array of faith centers, each with the capacity to touch the lives of their neighbors. The effect would be contagious—all of Catholic life would be charged with a closeness to Christ and a passionate desire to bring Christ to others. Not only would this transform our personal lives and the lives of our Catholic families. It would also spill over to the parish community.

That is where our handbook takes us now: to the parish and its particular abilities to reach out in the name of Christ.

### Reflection: Personal Evangelization

*God haunts few of us the way he haunted Paul.*

*His unique call led him to journeys, and the dangers of journeys, that stunned the Christian world of his day and laid down a pattern of passionate restlessness that still shapes our Catholic imagination.*

*Yet his missionary life came down to individual moments, personal moments, thresholds that he felt invited to cross. His prayer, his reflections, his contacts, his knowledge of roads and trade routes—all pressed him forward, to the next city, the next culture, the next continent. But most of all, to the next person who, unknowingly, awaited the encounter with Paul.*

*Paul was haunted even by his dreams.*

*Having walked, rode, sailed and caravanned through most of what we today call the Middle East and Turkey, Paul rested for a moment, leaving space for yet one more invitation from God, a dream.*

*In his dream, on the edge of "Asia," across from "Europe," at the Bosporus Strait that divided one ancient world from another, he sees a man and hears a voice.*

*"Come across, Paul," the man says, gesturing with his hand. Come to a new world. Come meet a new person. Open for Christ yet one more soul.*

*Paul wakens from his dream, now knowing how powerfully God pressed upon him.*

*Shaking off his weariness, he refuses to shake off the dream and its meaning.*

*Now others, unknowingly, await him: Corinthians, Philippians, Romans. Now others await him, one person at a time, until the Word of God encircles the globe.*

*(See Acts 16:9–10.)*

# Chapter 3

---

# PARISH EVANGELIZATION

For some, the notion of "parish evangelization" might seem almost contradictory. They might think, "*Parishes* don't evangelize; *individual people* do." But parishes are faith communities composed of individual people, all of whom have been baptized into Jesus Christ. In Catholic life, parish community, where the eucharist is celebrated and so much of Christian life is organized and supported, creates the indispensable background for individual evangelization.

We Catholics do not think of our parishes as somewhat arbitrary assemblies—collections of people who just happen to be together or who just happen to choose to be together. We think of, and define, our parishes as stable communities with the eucharist as their center (see the Code of Canon Law, #515.1). We Catholics believe that Christ saves us by calling us into community through baptism and by sustaining us through the worship of the community in the eucharist.

Of course, the eucharist means more than simply "having Mass." The eucharist, which the Second Vatican Council called the "source and summit" of our Christian life, involves so much: the call of God's Word in our lives, the vibrant worship of God through a variety of ministries and gifts, the empowerment of each member for mission, and the pledge of loving service for each other and the world, which is a sign of the coming of the Kingdom of God for which we long.

Being a eucharistic community, then, means living in response to God's Word, growing in ministry, committing ourselves to service and living in this world with hope for the Kingdom. In other words, our parish life means that we are disciples. The reform of the eucharist these past thirty years has worked toward one principal pastoral effect: to reinforce the life of discipleship in every Catholic. This is why we can speak of the "call to holiness" as coming to every baptized person, who is, by that sacrament, a disciple of Jesus Christ. Parish life, therefore, serves this discipleship, this call to growth in holiness.

If the parish's center is the eucharist, its burden does not stop when Mass is ended. Rather, one of the purposes of the Mass is to call us to service beyond the Mass itself in service to others. The word *Mass* comes from the Latin word *missa*—it derives from the idea of "sending" and "being sent."

Evangelization springs from the eucharist because, empowering us to be Christ's living body and spirit (think of the third eucharistic prayer: "Make us one body and one spirit in Christ"), it asks us to live for each other and for the world. That is exactly the framework for a Catholic who evangelizes: the invitation of Christ to his saving life, his empowering table, his community of disciples.

Because the eucharist is at the heart of Catholic life, parish plays a central role in evangelization. *Go and Make Disciples* expressly states that even if someone evangelizes one-to-one, he or she always has the table of the Lord as the referent: "When an individual evangelizes, one to one, he or she should have the Good News and the eucharistic table as the ultimate focus."

This is the evangelizing pattern for Catholics: we go forth from, and return to, the table.

## *The Challenge of Goal II*

Of all the goals and objectives proposed for Catholics by the bishops of the United States in *Go and Make Disciples,* the most difficult one for parishes to enact revolves around Goal II, the "outward-looking goal." Objectives that Goal II calls for—like inviting others to our parish, inviting people to the Catechumenate, welcoming inactive and marginal Catholics, trying to reach people who have no church, empowering our parishioners to be missionaries to reach the "other"—can easily stump even the most active parishes.

After all, the scope of Goal II is not tiny. The U.S. bishops ask us "to invite every person in the United States, whatever his or her cultural background, to hear the message of salvation in Jesus Christ, so they may come to join us in the fullness of the Catholic faith." When parishioners hear this, they think, "Every person is to be invited?" And they sit stunned. "How are we ever going to do that?" they ask themselves.

This goal, which lays such a broad and clear ideal before Catholics, does not mean, of course, that Catholics suspend the basic respect and encounter-basis of evangelization. By that very notion, it especially forbids Catholics to be ecumenically insensitive when spreading faith. Quite the contrary. The ecumenical movement finds its place in an evangelizing vision because, through it, the Holy Spirit brings the power of the Good News to bear upon all believers who are challenged to become brothers and sisters in the one family of Christ. Chapter 5 will look at these ecumenical issues at greater length. Even with ecumenical sensitivity, however, this goal still gives Catholics the sense that a lot has been laid on them.

However this goal makes Catholics feel, it certainly calls them beyond the simple routines of their parish life.

## Why Parishes Don't Reach Out

There are two clear reasons why this "outward-looking goal" is so difficult for parishes to live out.

First of all, parishes preoccupy themselves basically with providing liturgy and educational activities. When we look at parish budgets, most of the parish's money goes to pay salaries or to maintain buildings—the resources that make it possible for a parish to worship and educate (children, for the most part, but also sometimes adults receive education). Because parishes must worship and educate, it is perfectly natural for parishes to see these as the most important needs that they have. Should a parish not take care of these essential ministries, it would be dead.

Second, the people envisioned by the "outward-looking goal" of evangelization are not easy to "see." Where do we find inactive Catholics? Where do we find the unchurched? How do we reach out to "those people out there"? These are the people who do not come when a parish simply opens its doors. So how does a parish reach them?

Parishes have reported trying to reach inactive Catholics, and, they say, "no one showed up," or "we could not find any." We know that there are inactive Catholics and unchurched people all around. Hardly a Catholic family has not experienced the phenomenon of some of its members "drifting away," or "becoming inactive." Likewise, polls taken of the American people show that almost 45 percent of the broader population are not regularly involved in church if certain behavioral criteria are used.

The problem, here, is one of perspective: we see those we are conditioned to see. We see people we know. It's hard to see people whom we are not looking for and do not yet know. It's hard to see people whose needs are not as visible as the needs of our parishioners who come on Sunday, put the envelope in the basket, occasionally even volunteer to serve in one way or another, and are able to make their complaints and needs known.

As a result, the "outward-looking" objectives will go unmet unless parishes adopt a very clear and particular intention to reach beyond their regular membership with the fuller agenda that God gives them, the agenda of becoming a parish community that brings Good News beyond its own walls.

### All Groups Tend to Look Inward

Catholics may seem more culpable than other church groups in the difficulty they have looking beyond themselves, but in reality it may be that most communities settle for the comfortably familiar rather than the unsettlingly unfamiliar. Perhaps Catholics succumb to this comfortably familiar a bit more easily than some other groups, but the truth is this: it takes a lot of energy to reach out and beyond ourselves. After all, was it not the power of the Holy Spirit in Pentecost that allowed the first disciples to leave the places where Jesus appeared in resurrection and finally bring the news of his resurrection to *the nations?* (See Acts 2:1–12.) It took, and takes, lots of energy.

God gives this same energy, the power of the Holy Spirit, in every era of the Church. The Holy Spirit, the agent of evangelization, wants to empower our parishes to be less comfortable with themselves and more in tune with the missionary dimension that lies at the heart of every parish.

The Holy Spirit brings a special gift to every Catholic and every Catholic parish: the ability to resist its inward-looking tendency and the capacity to transcend its natural "inertia." We all know what inertia sounds like: "We never did this before; it has never been tried." Inertia is comfortable, as comfortable as defining community as "those people we know."

## Can Parishes Reach Out?

Because of Catholic parishes' natural difficulty in "looking outward," the whole task of bringing Good News to the "other" seems impossible. "How do we do this?" parishes ask. How do parishes go about doing what they are not naturally organized to do?

There are two answers to this. (1) Parishes almost inevitably need evangelization teams to help them maintain a good balance in their "inward-outward" focus. (2) Parishes need to learn some new behaviors and incorporate these behaviors into their ordinary parish life. (Chapter 4 will give some pointers for evangelization teams.)

*Go and Make Disciples* envisioned some behaviors being adopted by parishes—inviting, welcoming, recruiting, canvassing, mailing, advertising, home visiting, and other ways to reach the inactive and the unchurched. When we look at this list, we see that some of these activities happen quite naturally in parish life. Is there a parish that doesn't mail? Is there a parish that hasn't at one point or another taken a census? Other activities may have been accomplished once upon a time in the past ("We had a Legion that visited homes"). Or certain kinds of outreach may be done for certain events ("We put a big sign up for the annual bazaar").

But most parishes, when it comes to evangelization, find that a disciplined set of ministries designed to reach out to nonmembers seems to escape them. They cannot quite bring it off. They revert to the familiar and the comfortable, taking care of their own parishioners.

Yet parishes that undertake the full work of evangelization, if they are able to galvanize both the personal and the parish aspects of this ministry, will find enormous energy throughout the whole pastoral life. In other words, nothing will so much take care of "our own" as helping the parish reclaim its missionary soul. So much energy emerges from seeing the power

of eucharist extended into the lives of others, or trying to
address the needs of those "lost sheep" who lie just outside the
pale of the parish's life, that parishes will find themselves in a
startling process of renewal.

## The Ordinary Life of Parish Evangelization

The point of this chapter has to be placed in the famework
of pastoral life. No outreach activity stands alone. We can hire
blimps to fly overhead, wire our parking lots with loudspeak-
ers, have dancing clowns on the front steps of our churches
and send a prize to every person living in our parish bound-
aries. Such efforts, however, are all the more ridiculous if they
do not emerge from a spirit nestled in the ordinary life of the
parish that has discovered evangelization at its core.

The first and third goals of *Go and Make Disciples* speak to
these ordinary, and necessary, ministries of evangelization.
The first goal talks about our ongoing renewal in God's Word
and Christ's worship, and our growth in faith as communities,
families and individuals. The *enthusiasm* we have for our faith
helps us to *share* it. The third goal points to the impact the
Gospel has to have on the world, society's values and the dignity of individuals, on our service to the poor and support of
our families, all as an indispensable part of evangelization.

To concentrate on the "outward-looking" aspects of evangelization presumes, then, these other ways that parishes
become evangelizing.

Parish catechetics, the RCIA Catechumenate, the Sunday
liturgy, adult religious education, family support, youth ministry, services for the poor, parish organizations and societies,
reconciliation services, baptismal and confirmation preparation, young adult outreach and marriage preparation, neighborhood involvement, hospital visitation—these and so many
other ministries of a parish make up the "usual" ways that
parishes will evangelize.

In view of clear trends from the early '90s that show dramatic rises in the numbers of adults received into the Catholic Church compared to the '70s and '80s, no parish can absolve itself from having a strong catechumenal process. There is an obvious connection between the establishment of the RCIA catechumenal ministry, spearheaded by the North American Forum on the Catechumenate, and the recent rise in adult converts. Parishes that try to talk evangelization while neglecting the formation of a Catechumenate will simply be left out of the conversation when it comes to an ecclesially centered evangelization.

The same kinds of observations can also be made about liturgical renewal in general, the formation of small Christian faith-sharing groups and compassionate outreach to inactive and alienated Catholics. Modern parishes of every size and financial situation are finding the ability to renew themselves and to extend their invitation beyond their own members. The ultimate process behind any successful parish is undoubtedly the same: members of a parish begin to see themselves as disciples and, with growing involvement in their faith, find the stimulus to reach out to others.

Goal II, with its challenge for parishes to look beyond themselves, presumes that parishes have a nucleus of ordinary ways in which people grow in faith and share it. The special emphasis of this chapter, the outreach strategies parishes need to develop, in no way ignores the ordinary way, through their life, that parishes evangelize. Rather, the purpose of this handbook is to expand and enlarge the built-in grace of parish evangelization by providing directions for those evangelizing activities that parishes often feel uncomfortable organizing. Because even with successful catechumenal programs, the question still remains: how do we more effectively inform people about the process of becoming a committed Catholic disciple, and how do we more urgently invite those, beyond our church walls, who are searching?

This third chapter of our handbook on evangelization will

provide ideas for certain outreach ministries. Specifically, we will look at welcoming, mailing and home visitation as activities that parishes can, without enormous pain, undertake. When these activities are adopted in the context of personal evangelization—the power of a Catholic's own continuing conversion and willingness to share his or her story of faith in appropriate ways—and in the context of the ordinary evangelizing life of a parish, they become resources by which Good News can begin to be felt outside the church's walls in the lives of inactive and unchurched neighbors.

When that starts to happen, then a parish will be beginning to live up to its call.

# WELCOME

Some of the severest irony that Jesus ever used toward a particular person in the Gospels revolved around how he was welcomed, or, to be exact, how he was not welcomed.

Simon, a prominent and respected Pharisee, invited Jesus to his house. While Jesus was seated with the guests at meal, a woman held in low esteem by others in the town entered Simon's house, approached Jesus, started weeping on Jesus' feet and wiping those feet with her tears. Simon was scandalized. If Jesus were a true prophet, thought Simon, he'd know what kind of woman this was at his feet.

Jesus, entirely capable of reading hearts, knew exactly what Simon, and probably most of the other guests, was thinking. So he decided to call Simon on his thoughts and judgments, and he did so by pointing out some startling differences. Simon gave Jesus no greeting when he arrived, but this woman had not stopped embracing the feet of Jesus. Simon provided no water for the traditional ceremonial washing, but Jesus' feet were being bathed by the tears of this woman. Nor did Simon provide anointing oil for Jesus, but this woman, held in such low opinion by the town, had poured precious oil on the feet of Jesus.

Simon, on the one hand, provided no welcome to Jesus; this sorrowful woman could not, on the other hand, stop honoring Jesus and showing her love (Lk 7:26–50).

Such vivid irony on the part of Jesus points out the very human dimensions that lie at the basis of the community and the Church to which Jesus calls us: the capacity to welcome and accept each other as human beings and as brothers and sisters.

## Welcoming Says a Lot About a Parish

We all know what it is like to visit another church, one different from our regular Sunday parish. Our antennae are fine-tuned. Our approach to the church and our entrance create subtle feelings in us. We examine our experiences—what's it like to find the church, to park, to enter the building, whether the lights are on, whether anyone greets us, whether people sit as far from each other as they can, how the people relate to each other, how they sing, how they attend to the liturgy of the word, how they approach the eucharist, and whether they cut each other off when leaving the parking lot after Mass.

These subtle ways that a community shows itself are also the most obvious indicators that a community has to show itself to others. What many parishioners hardly notice shouts loudly to the visitor.

These indicators send out vibrations that lead people to feel attracted toward, neutral about or repulsed by a particular parish. Perhaps we judge that these are weak or irrelevant criteria, but the truth about contemporary society is that people love options and will exercise them as often as they can. Modern society gives people choices. If they don't like one place, they can go to another. If they prefer one thing, they can bypass everything else. Our churches cannot be exempt from this process either.

The subtle ways we welcome people stand out like large,

irrefutable gestures that say either "embrace" or "cold shoulder" to those who come to us.

## Seeing How We Look

Because the ways we welcome are so subtle, they can be particularly hard for ordinary parishioners to clearly recognize. Many Catholics go to church on automatic pilot. They have their routines down, and unfortunately, many are oblivious of how they treat, or do not treat, others. Parishioners come to see themselves as "insiders" and take for granted the kinds of signals they send and receive when they go to church.

This produces the phenomenon of very devout Catholics who are so absorbed with attending to the divine presence in the tabernacle that they will not move three feet and let their fellow parishioner into the pew. And eager ushers who, with a dour face, hand out collection envelopes as their welcoming gesture to parishioners and guests as they arrive for worship. And talented musicians who insist on tuning and retuning their instruments as people are gathering. And frugal pastors who keep the church dark until twenty seconds before Mass is to begin. And chatty parishioners who, liberated from the "keep silent in church" injunctions of the past, insist on transmitting the latest versions of neighborhood gossip in stage whispers while others are trying to recollect themselves before Mass starts.

It is hard for us to see the signals we send and receive.

As a result, parish leadership—particularly those involved in Sunday worship (pastors, staff, pastoral council, finance council, lectors and eucharistic ministers)—has to train itself to clearly see itself, to see its parish as visitors or strangers might see it. Since it is so hard to see how our own congregation assembles, a good strategy is to use visits to other congregations as a foil to our own experience.

## Checking Others Out

An ongoing exercise we might employ in our parishes would be to send parish leadership out every six months or so to drop in on other congregations with an inventory of factors to watch for. If our congregation has parish leadership that travels quite a bit, then such an inventory can be taken along as part of their "travel equipment." Then every so often part of a parish meeting can be given over to surveying the results of this informal inventory of other congregations and applying them to our own parishes.

An inventory of factors might include:

- Was it easy to follow signs to the church? Why?
- What was it like to park?
- What did we experience when we entered the door of the church?
- Were there greeters? How did they act?
- What were ushers, lectors, eucharistic ministers, celebrants and others doing before the Mass began?
- Was special notice taken of visitors? How was this done?
- What was the ambiance of the congregation? How did it make one feel? Why?
- Did the congregation sing? How did it follow the readings?
- How did the congregation approach receiving communion?
- What happened as Mass ended?
- Was there any fellowship after the Mass? What was it like?
- How did the congregation act in the parking lot?

A congregation that learns to notice these things in other assemblies will be, in effect, studying these factors in itself.

It is extremely important here to recognize that every congregation is different and that no hard-and-fast rule can be laid down for every single parish. The size, locale, style and number of staff persons in a parish can all make for significant differences in the kind of assembly style a parish has. Nevertheless, every parish will be sending signals about itself; the better it can come to interpret these signals, the closer it can come to the New Testament ideal of being a community of welcome.

Parishes can review two aspects of welcoming as they examine themselves: (1) how they welcome their own members and (2) how they welcome others.

WELCOMING OUR OWN MEMBERS

There's no point in discussing how we welcome visitors and strangers if we have not looked at how we welcome ourselves—namely, how the assembly gathers and what kind of welcome we give each other when we come together. We cannot let the size of our parishes absolve us from thinking about this; some of the largest church communities in the United States, the self-styled "megachurches," manage to make every one of the participants (usually in a crowd of thousands) feel welcomed and at home.

In welcoming our own members, two particular situations come to mind: (a) the way we greet new parishioners and (b) the way we greet each other at Mass and other occasions. Each of these greetings clearly portrays our parish's sense of community and the quality of its assembly.

## Welcoming New Parishioners

Pastoral staffs and evangelization teams need to be made aware of the personal and social impact that moving has on today's society. Because families and individuals move so frequently, moving from one locale to another is the single largest predictor of becoming inactive in church. The reason is obvious: one leaves a parish that is quite familiar and probably full of precious life memories; so finding a new parish has one strike already against it—it will not be familiar and will seem necessarily impersonal. It will not seem like "home."

What can be done about this?

- Our methods of "registering new parishioners" have to be reviewed and humanized. All too often people are given tired-looking forms to fill out, forms with impersonal or all-too-personal information...and that's the end of it. Except, of course, for receiving envelopes. Not much of a welcome here.

- Our parishes must find ways to identify new members and be sure there is some personal contact on the part of the parish with these people, to the extent that they want personal contact. (Some, no matter how we try, simply will not want any more contact than their name on a list.) Can we find parishioners who can make these personal contacts with newcomers, even if only by phone?

- People, when they register, need to be invited into the parish family. At the very least, this means communicating some basic information about the parish to the new registrant. It should, ideally, also be a way to invite new people into the ministries and opportunities for community that a parish has.

- Registration should also take into account any special needs that new parishioners might have—people sick at home, children who need day care or a "nursery" service during liturgy, social or economic needs that make a special claim on the parish community.

- New parishioners should also be directly welcomed into a special gathering just for them. At this gathering (it could be a simple reception, or perhaps a small lunch or dinner), new parishioners not only get to meet each other; they meet the pastor and pastoral staff, as well as others who exercise leadership in the diocese. These gatherings, done quite successfully in many parishes today, should be conducted several times a year (depending, of course, on the number of new registrations). A "reminder" call to the homes (fortunately most people today have answering machines) will insure a dramatically higher number of attendees.

- Set up a "welcoming table" at the Sunday Masses; the frequency can depend on parish needs. Invite visitors and new parishioners to visit the table to receive information about the parish. New parishioners can also learn about the process of registering and becoming involved in the parish from those who staff the tables.
- In addition, parishes should consider a welcoming ceremony during one of the Masses. Liturgists in the parish should be able to design something that makes a lot of sense and does not subvert the basic pattern of worship that people expect on Sunday. (For that matter, parishioners who are moving away might also be well served by some blessing or special designation at a liturgy.)

## Greeting Each Other at Mass

The other aspect of "welcoming our own members" has to do with the way we greet parishioners when they gather. Much experimentation has been done by various parishes in the past decade, most of it with good results. The following are some points for pastoral leadership and evangelization teams to consider:

- Is the parish accessible to people, particularly those with special physical needs or those who are aging?
- Would the parish benefit by some kind of greeting ministry? Many parishes have found parishioners eager to stand by the door on Sunday and welcome other parishioners, and also visitors and newcomers.
- Hold a training session for the ushers of the parish, alerting them to the kinds of people who visit the church and how the ushers can be of help to those who come to the church on Sunday. Ushers should be very aware of their importance in creating an immediate sense of the parish for those entering the church building. (If the ushers, for

example, are all outside the front door smoking, it gives off a distinct message to the churchgoers.)

- Have a way for people to recognize and identify each other by name, whether before Mass, at the beginning of Mass, or if the congregation is small enough, by name badges that parishioners put on when they come to church. (If you have badges, be sure to have special identifying tags or badges for visitors, or else they will particularly feel left out.)
- Make hospitality true hospitality after the Masses. Parishes today, when they renovate or build a new structure, routinely include informal gathering space. Many parishes also hold "coffee and donut" sessions after some or all of their Masses. Often, however, these sessions degenerate into a scene like this: a few parishioners greet the few other parishioners they know—and ignore anyone else they do not know. Make sure those who organize hospitality circulate among the people, clearly identifying visitors or people they have not yet met. Naturally, attendance at these by the pastor and pastoral staff should be mandatory.
- At other gatherings (meetings, education sessions, service projects, etc.), make sure everyone has been introduced and knows others at the gathering. So often we presume knowledge of each other when the fact is that people are sitting in our midst without the slightest idea of who is beside them.

WELCOMING OTHERS

It may, sadly, come as a surprise to many Catholics that there actually are, in their congregations Sunday after Sunday, visitors and strangers.

So often regular churchgoers put on "blinders" that enable them to see only people they already know or, even worse, to ignore just about anyone else. When this is a collective mentality, visitors and strangers can be little more than onlookers. While many might prefer just to be onlookers, those who are looking for a new parish or have questions or an interest in joining the Catholic Church are left to fend for themselves.

Every congregation should be constantly aware that visitors may (and probably are) in their midst and, therefore, our congregations have a responsibility for them.

In addition to those who come as visitors to Mass, many others move into neighborhoods and live next to Catholic neighbors or even on the same block as the Catholic Church. Others avail themselves of one or another service of the parish (homeless shelter, counseling, adult education class) either on-site or away from the parish plant.

Both these groups, those who come as visitors on Sunday and those who are near to us, deserve to feel a welcome from our parish congregations.

## *Sunday Visitors*

Informal conversation reveals a rather predictable anecdote: when people visit Protestant churches, they report always getting "special treatment." They were recognized as visitors, greeted personally by those around them, asked to sign a visitors' book and often received a follow-up letter from the pastor.

We can be sure that this is not true of every Protestant congregation, but this is reported frequently enough to give us pause: can it be that there is a whole etiquette, a whole method of greeting visitors to our parishes, that we Catholics simply have not caught on to? This feeling that we are missing out on something basic, along with the sense that our parishes generally put out a cold shoulder, combines to raise some fundamental questions for every Catholic congregation.

Although we never really know how many "visitors" are in our pews, we all know that just about everyone in the RCIA catechumenal program was once just such a visitor, coming as a stranger to our church. Even though we advertise far and wide for "inactive Catholics," we know that most people who show up at "listening sessions" our parishes might run were actually tentatively exploring a return to the Church by "sneaking a peek" at our parish on Sunday mornings.

There obviously are extremes in welcoming visitors: people do not want to be embarrassed or feel prevailed upon. But to tell the truth, most Catholic parishes are far from getting near this danger.

What might parishes do for visitors who come on Sunday?

- Does our parish have a visitors' sign-in book with a place for addresses and remarks?
- Does our parish have an appropriate way to recognize and/or introduce visitors? (This depends a lot on the culture and size of the parish.)
- Has our parish developed an attractive brochure about our church, one designed specifically for visitors and guests? (This kind of brochure should in no way be confused with those general parish brochures that endlessly list organizations and programs of the parish and end up looking rather like phone books. That kind of brochure makes a lot of sense for those who already know the parish, but it is simply mumbo jumbo to visitors.)
- What kind of "visitor card" or "visitor envelope" have we designed for our pews on Sunday? (A card, by the way, might be much better than an envelope, which carries the implication that it's for "money" rather than communication.) A simple, attractive card asking basic information can be easily designed and left in the pews or back of church.
- Have we figured out a way to make sure visitors are greeted during "coffee and donut" hospitality time?
- Do we have a standard follow-up letter to thank visitors who come to our church and to ask if there's anything our parish can do for them?

- Have we trained our parishioners about what to do when they bring someone (friend or relative) as a guest to our church?
- Might we set aside occasional Sundays when parishioners are *encouraged* to bring visitors (friends and coworkers) to our parish just to visit and be recognized?

These are just beginning ideas for what a pastoral council or evangelization team might do to facilitate those who come visiting at our parish churches.

### Neighbors

Parishes exist in neighborhoods and, when we think about the instability of today's modern life, often are the only abiding and structuring institution in their neighborhood. As such, they play a role in how people think of their neighborhoods, a role of helping surrounding neighbors identify with their locale in personal and social ways. Even if people do not care one bit about church, they can often identify with "the big church on Main Street" or the "pretty church that has an after-school program." These forms of identification help modern people organize their life around human and recognizable patterns; our parishes provide oases in the midst of endless highways with clusters of suburban houses or anonymous high-rises with boxlike apartments.

Yet our parishes often shrink from neighborhood roles. So often are parishes wrapped up with their own agenda that only a major crisis jolts them into doing something in and with the neighborhood—a problem with drugs, gangs, theft or some such thing. That our parishes can actually be giving leadership in and with our neighborhoods dawns on only a few of the clergy and active laypeople.

There is a whole ministry to neighborhoods and to neighbors

that can often lead to the enriching of the lives of others; it can also be the seedbed for drawing people to Christ and his Church.

A ministry to neighbors might include some of the following:

- Selected home visitation when new housing is built or ownership changes.
- Preparation of "welcome packets" for those who move into our neighborhood. Such packets can contain information about our town or area, important phone numbers, references to local houses of worship, and information about our own parish.
- Involvement in certain neighborhood associations, followed up by regular reports to the pastor and the pastoral council.
- Development of particular brochures about our parish, created with the "non-Catholic neighbor" in mind.
- Festivals and celebrations in which the "whole neighborhood" is involved. The pre-Christmas season and the patronal feast of the parish are two such festival times that offer special opportunities.
- Concerts, organ recitals, musical programs, plays and talent shows that reach out beyond our own membership.
- Adoption of the responsibility for fulfilling a certain neighborhood need by your parish. Some of this might extend all the way from litter removal to a soup kitchen ministry.
- Listing of the parish in the lobbies of nearby hotels and motels.
- A parish-sponsored bus pickup service to and from certain nursing homes or housing projects.

## Parishioners Want to Welcome

Parishes should not at all feel at a loss when it comes to welcoming. With just a bit of probing, pastors will find that parishioners are eager to welcome and would love a way to give input into this important ministry, which derives right from the Scriptures.

Any parish can test the waters by asking for helpers who have an interest in making the parish "more welcoming." Pastors and staff will be surprised at how many will actually show up for such a planning meeting simply because so many Catholics feel embarrassed about the lack of appropriate welcome parishes often give. It is, they have concluded, one of the great absences in parish life. If given a chance, Catholics will tell story after story of how hard it was for them to "break into" their new parish, so that, as a result, they have a vested interest in changing that.

Sitting down with a group of parishioners who want to work on welcoming, pastors and staff persons can proceed by simply conducting an open brainstorm session, beginning with anecdotal impressions that parishioners have, and moving through consideration of the major welcoming issues that a parish faces: welcoming its own members, new members, visitors, neighbors or other special categories of people that make a particular claim on the parish. Once the brainstorming is done, parishioners will be eager to take on different aspects of the most solid suggestions for a welcoming ministry, designing approaches and providing resources so that this fundamental need in the parish is met.

Parishes will be pleasantly surprised at how much enthusiasm there is for greeting others in the name of Christ. It's an untapped, and buoyant, fountain of energy.

## PUBLIC RELATIONS AND MAILINGS

We need to begin this section on public relations and mailings by setting the record straight, clearly articulating two basic truths about Catholic evangelization:

1. The most powerful energy for evangelization is prayer.
2. The greatest publicity a parish will ever have is its own

congregation. Nothing will communicate invitation, welcome and sharing more than an actual, living, breathing Catholic who has the ability to appropriately involve others in conversations about faith.

In view of this, everything in this chapter presumes these two truths about prayer and discipleship. If we lose sight of this, we inevitably reduce evangelization to "slick marketing" and abstract programs that some "experts" take charge of—the very opposite of the Catholic vision of evangelization.

Evangelization, to repeat the point, is not an extraordinary activity that a few overly enthused people do, but the ordinary activity of every Catholic in every parish. The more we situate evangelization in the hands of the "enthused" (whether those considered religiously fanatical or those considered marketing specialists), the more we take away the power of the average Catholic to experience his or her ability to "bring Christ to every human situation," as the U.S. Catholic bishops put it.

After we acknowledge these two basic truths, however, is there a place for publicity and mailing in Catholic evangelization? Are there benefits to be gained, presuming the ever necessary role of prayer and discipleship?

## The Value of a Tool

The benefits to be gained by public relations and mailing have to be correctly weighed. Because these, and other strategies, basically supplement and support the ongoing evangelization that takes place between believers and searchers, our trouble comes about when we cease thinking of these strategies as tools and start thinking of them as the heart of evangelization. We then begin placing on them a weight that they cannot bear. We begin expecting them to do far more than what they can do. And we, once again, substitute an abstraction for the direct encounter that constitutes evangelization.

Publicity strategies, as tools, are limited in what they can do. Using them effectively means acknowledging those limitations and being content with the restricted effectiveness they can have. Every one of us would love to find that "magic wand" of evangelization that "works"—presto!—to convert the world. It simply does not exist. The more we go searching for it, the more we waste our time.

One way to understand the limitations of various strategies in evangelization is through acknowledging a "fundamental law" of sharing. The law goes like this:

**A response will only be in direct proportion
to the invitation.**

Let's explore this for a moment. Think about the hundreds of things we are asked to respond to in the course of a day, whether TV/radio ads, telephone calls, e-mail and "snail mail," invitations to lunch or dinner, shopping lists, children's cries, hugs and whispers, sitcoms and dramas, the evening news, the front doorbell or noises from the neighbors' window.

To these and hundreds of other stimuli, we make choices to respond, sometimes automatically, sometimes reluctantly, sometimes with enthusiasm. But those choices we most vividly and clearly make involve people who directly ask a response from us, whose faces we plainly see and whose reactions we can directly gauge. The more personal the invitation, the more personal our response can be. When our child is crying, we engage directly with that child. When the checkout person smiles at us, we smile back. Direct invitation invites direct response.

To the indirect messages of our lives, we have the choice of not responding without any risk, or responding on our terms. But to direct invitations, given in person, we almost have to respond; only rarely can we put these aside without any consequences. Something has been asked of us, personally; we have to make some response.

When we look at publicity, however, we note right away that it does not involve a direct invitation. It is indirect, almost by definition. As a result, people have the freedom to respond indirectly, abstractly, by choosing or refusing, without any risk or consequences.

For this reason, the tools of publicity will always have built-in limitations. Once evangelization teams recognize this, however, they can then appreciate the limited, but clear, advantages that publicity efforts can bring about.

## *What Are the Advantages?*

There is a church in New York City that places a television monitor just within its front garden gate. Using standard personal computer presentation software, it presents on the street a string of images and messages to those who walk by. It is a busy corner, far busier now than when the television monitor was first put up. At that time over 150 persons walked in front of the church every hour. The number of passersby is probably more than double at this time.

Initiatives like this make all of us think about those hundreds, every hour, walking by our own church building. Consider how we ourselves walk by buildings and windows, or how we drive down boulevards and avenues. Does anything catch our attention? Why? What does it mean when something does stand out?

Even more, why is it so hard for our churches to stand out at all? That is so obvious, isn't it? Our churches, like our broader Catholic population, look quite invisible, even when they are massive edifices or sit atop dominating hills. Our buildings get to look much like the furniture in our house: they are taken for granted and, therefore, unnoticed.

Publicity works against this tendency toward taking things for granted and making the familiar look anonymous. It gives some sense of distinction, of standing out, some more vivid or direct connection between a person and our parish. It helps people draw some line between their everyday experience and our parish community.

Because the truth is that people walk or drive in front of our churches but they have no sense of what we are doing inside these buildings or what our faith community stands for. The intensity, power and spirituality that organizes our Catholic life lies hidden to the rest of the world. This results in a tragedy: that millions are searching for a spiritual home, for a community of faith, and they just do not see us.

## Basic Publicity

A pastoral staff or evangelization team does not have to wander very far to begin thinking about basic publicity for their parish. As in the area of welcoming, some visits to other churches and congregations might open our eyes to the pros and cons of our own parish's presentation of itself. When we've driven around the block three times looking for some other church's main office, we begin to think about how invisible our own front offices might be.

Here is a checklist of some basic publicity points to check out:

- What kind of sign announces our church to its neighborhood? What message is on it? Is the sign visible and attractive? Are there other signs that compete with this basic sign (e.g., the infamous and ubiquitous "Bingo" sign) and dull its power? Are there words of welcome and invitation on the sign? Is there so much information on it that people cannot easily comprehend it?
- How accessible are the main offices of our church? We should think of physical accessibility right off the top because, when offices are out of the physical reach of

others, we have already made a big negative statement about our parish. Beyond physical accessibility, are the parish offices clearly marked? The message we put on this sign can say many things, some inadvertent: "The clergy do not want to see you"; "The pastoral staff maintains strict hours to keep from being bothered"; "The hours are for the convenience of our employees and not our parishioners." We want to be sure not to be saying messages like this.

- What is our reception area like? Is it pleasant to sit in? Do people feel isolated in it? When people are waiting there, are they inflicted with all kinds of things that can make them ill at ease, like chats between the clergy and receptionist, or private conversations between the receptionist and her family, or the rattle of office machines?
- What is our reception like? How are people greeted when they call or visit? What kind of etiquette sets the tone for our reception ministry? Often parishes unintentionally give off the "Father doesn't want to talk to you" message just by the tone used when someone calls. Sure, a receptionist has to appropriately do some screening and referring–why else have one? But how that is done can make a world of difference. In this regard, what message do we send by having teens staff our reception areas after hours?
- What are the front doors of our church like? Are they easy to enter? Do they strain the backs of our elderly parishioners, or test the muscles of preteens? Some church doors are designed so that they somehow always look closed. Often our churches do not have clear times posted about when the doors are open or even clear procedures for getting them open (leaving parishioners gathered outside church early in the morning wondering how to open the church when the sacristan or the priest is late).
- What kinds of literature do we have in our church vestibule? Here we might consider literature about our

parish in general, about various ministries that seek to reach out to others, and literature about the Catholic faith. If we have ministries designed for visitors or newcomers, these should be highlighted in a particular way—the RCIA, ministries for returning Catholics, youth outreach efforts, young adult and young married programs, senior meetings, etc. While we have to be cautious not to "junk up" our vestibules, we should not be afraid to highlight specific items.

- We could also review our church bulletins, examining them from the point of view of a "visitor" or "outsider." What does the bulletin say about your church? How does it come off in terms of evangelization and invitation? What is prominent on the front cover, and what impression does that give? Are all the messages about money and fund-raising? Just imagine the impression given if the bulletin contains notices about bingo, a parish Las Vegas night, trips to the local casino and a raffle for the youth group. None of this is bad in itself, but together, what message gets across? Does the bulletin locate things in the context of word, worship, community and service? Does it have endless announcements from parish and nonparish groups that only confuse people? Pastoral staffs should recognize that the parish bulletin is the instrument that most consistently communicates an impression, good or bad, by the parish to its members and to others.

- Does your parish have a brochure for visitors and guests? If so, what is in it? Does it read like a parish phone book, or does it clearly portray the images and commitments of your parish in accord with your parish mission statement? How is this brochure distributed or made available? We might examine it particularly for the overall impression it conveys by its titles, images and photos. We also need to test this, and all parish public relations, by its ability to communicate with our parishioners and our neighborhood; does it, for example, use Spanish or Korean if that's who lives in our neighborhood?

Some time spent in "inventory" of the basic publicity that our parish uses can yield a ready and great result. At the very least, it can identify those parts of our public relations that actually work against our parish and inadvertently blur its image. Most probably, such an inventory will help us sharpen and heighten the kind of message that our parish most wants to present to its members and to nonmembers as well.

## MAILING

The issue of "direct" and "indirect" invitation comes to the forefront when we think about mailing. Every one of us gets mail almost every day. Over 800,000 people are dedicated to bringing letters and packages to virtually everyone in our country. With mail we can even get an international reach, extending our message to virtually anywhere in the world. The U.S. Postal Service can give us a variety of delivery services, from first-class mail through third-class bulk mail; competitors with the U.S. Postal Service offer us next-day service of letters and packages. When we think about it, mail delivery is one of the most reliable and predictable forms of communication— and one of the cheapest.

Yet all this hype about the wonders of mail starts to fail when we consider the ways we actually open our mail. We notice this particularly if we have been away from home for a few days or longer, but this situation only underscores the way we sort and dispose of our daily mail. We certainly do not treat all pieces of mail equally, and once we get jaded, we can be pretty selective about what postal items are opened and read.

While not everyone moves near a trash can when opening mail, many of us do! And many of us routinely dump into the trash almost all our bulk mail, including those impressive four-color jobs that advertisers paid a lot of money for with the "guarantee" that they would get our attention. Catalogues, on which companies expended millions, may or, most probably, may not get saved. A few people rescue letters from nonprofits with desperate writing on the front: *OPEN IMMEDIATELY, URGENT, YOU CAN HELP.* Most people trash those as well, particularly if they are from charities that one has not planned donating to.

After we have done the initial screening and our mail has gotten down to the pile that really interests us, we still sort it some more. Bills often do not get opened right away; once a month, when we pay our bills, is enough. Other first-class mail gets prioritized as well: letters with stamps rank higher than those with meter impressions; letters with handwriting make more claim than letters with labels; and letters from those we know, of a personal nature, usually get opened first.

Every organization that uses the mail has to be aware that this is the kind of competition it faces. Every group that uses the mail has to be absolutely clear that a lot of what is mailed will end up unopened, particularly if it seems impersonal. Every parish that uses mail also has to be content with the observation that results from a mailing may never seem comparable to the work it takes printing, stuffing, addressing, stamping and posting. After all, when we work so hard, there must be a rewarding result, right? It unfortunately doesn't work that way.

Yet, even when all these limitations in mailing are admitted, the fact remains that mailing is the most ready and cost-effective way to place new ideas and new images before a large audience. To do the mailing ministry effectively, parishes must be content with this practical limit:

> **Through the mail we have an opportunity to place fresh ideas and images before other people. Whether sooner or later, some people will act on those ideas and images. But mail will not always produce directly observable results.**

As we shall see, not all mailings are alike, but parishes have to be content to live with the limitations of mailing, or else they will miss out on the many possibilities of mailing. Because mail, whether we can see the results or not, does put other images into the hands of many people. Eventually, some people will act on those images. But that process is largely up to them. Think of it as seed sown, like the Gospel parable; we sow a lot of seed that may come to flower at some point. But if the seed is not sown freely and far, it is not likely to have any effect at all.

## Mailing to Those We Know

Of the two kinds of mailing a parish might conduct, to people who are known and to people who are unknown, the more effective mailing will be to the first group—those whose names we have and who are, on one level or another, known.

Unfortunately, parishes almost entirely ignore the possibilities of mailings to these parishioners, even though it is the easiest kind of mailing that a parish might do. These are parishioners whose names and addresses the parish already has. These people have already been to the parish and, to one extent or another, identify with it. To reach these people, all a parish needs to do is:

- open a database
- select the group desired
- compose mail
- put on postage and send it

There are groups of parishioners who might be somewhat peripheral to the parish, for whom the right piece of mail might make a big difference. Even though it is relatively easy to assemble credible lists of parishioners who would benefit by hearing from the parish, parishes still continue to go about their routine activities and continue to overlook the possibilities of simple mailings that are easily at their disposal.

But the parish's readiness to do some focused mailing touches only one half of the equation; the other half involves those who will receive the mail and what their attitudes might be. One frequently reported downside to parish mailing concerns the tendency of people to "put aside" parish mailing because, when they see the return address of the parish, they presume that the letter concerns raising funds. As a result, they leave the envelope unopened.

Two strategies might counteract this negative reaction: (1) the parish might do more mailings that do not involve fund-raising, and (2) the parish can put something on the outside of the envelope to suggest that this is not a fund-raising effort. Phrases like "A Message for Our Friends," or "We're Keeping in Touch," or "We Have Good News for You," or other such sentiments might dispose someone to open a parish envelope that otherwise might sit unopened on a shelf.

What are the kinds of groups that parish mailings might help?

- parents of the recently baptized
- relatives of the recently deceased
- those recently visited in the hospital
- those newly registered in the parish
- parents of school or religious education children
- students going off to/returning from college
- youth and/or young adults
- parish ministers, particularly after a hard task was accomplished
- those who seem suddenly "inactive" in the parish
- those who seem to have stopped coming to church altogether

Once we start realizing the numbers of people who might benefit from some regular contact with the parish, our imaginations will quickly gravitate to other groups whom the parish also might well contact.

## What's Our Good News?

Each group that we reach out to has different needs. So when the parish decides to write to these groups, it has to, first of all, address the needs that are clearly present. In other words, it has to think about the agenda of those it is contacting before it thinks about its own agenda.

This does not mean that its own agenda disappears. But that agenda cannot be readily heard by busy or stressed people unless they get the feeling that their needs, concerns and situations are understood and, as a result, a dialogue is possible. When writing to parents today, for example, the parish has to be aware of the enormous pressures on today's parents simply in terms of time. Many households have both parents working, and if they are professionals, they work ten or more hours a day. What kind of mailing, a parish has to ask itself, will help this group? How would it look if the parish seemed ignorant of the basic constraints on their lives? Parishes have to recognize the agendas of those with whom they want to share.

After doing this, when the parish then tries to communicate its agenda, it has to think positive. It has to think "good news." It has to be conscious of the positive motivating factors behind allegiance to church today—family, community, service, quest for values and meaning. If a parish can present itself with these positive values, it will speak much louder than the usual "institutionalese" that parishes keep putting out as if it were religiously relevant.

There is little need, for example, to berate people one is trying to contact. Sometimes pastors and parish leaders do this in subtle ways that they consider clever, but actually only further the feeling that "we are the Church; we don't need you, you need us." For example, someone reported a priest saying on

Easter morning as he surveyed the bulging congregation, "Well, I see that Jesus was not the only one to rise this day." A very witty line, to be sure, but how was it heard? We can be this way in many of our communications—self-righteous and judgmental.

Without wanting to, we can be quite put-offish by sending signals to those we almost unconsciously consider inactive, lazy, unconcerned about faith, uncommitted, sinful, weak, opportunistic or angry. We dismiss them ahead of time by our attitudes. We keep "sticking it to them." We think that guilt and shame will convince people when, in today's world, guilt trips just send people somewhere else.

Bear in mind that we are concerned here with people who are likely to be not yet "on board" with reference to the parish or involvement in church. These people do not need all four sections of the Catechism dumped on their head. After people start to get involved, there will be plenty of opportunity to give direction. But first they need to be involved. Mark, the evangelist, shows Jesus using an analogous strategy: he speaks in parables to the "crowds," but to his own inner disciples he speaks of his upcoming death. (See Mk 5:33–34.)

## What to Send

With today's computers and photocopying shops, every parish has ready opportunity to produce decent-looking materials for mailing without expending a tremendous amount of money. Of course, because we mail so little, *any* amount of money can seem excessive. But it really isn't, not when one considers the number of people one might reach for relatively little expense. Today it should be possible to design and print up something simple for less than ten cents a piece; postage adds, depending on how one organizes it, the major chunk of the expense.

But if the mailing list is limited, these rates are not too much for a parish to bear. Suppose, for example, a parish baptized fifty children last year. Suppose (and this might be asking too much) the parish also kept a database of the parents of those children. To mail all those parents, even if it cost fifty cents a piece, would only amount to $25.00, the price of two good pizzas.

A quick list of things that can be mailed are:

- personalized letters
- general "Dear Parishioner" letters
- newsletters
- brochures
- newspapers
- material produced by others (e.g., articles or updates)
- small gifts or mementos
- calendars
- parish bulletins

As one analyzes whom the parish is trying to reach, differ-ent kinds of material make more sense for different groups. For example, only personalized letters should go to the grieving and to those who recently came out of the hospital. Simple, warm, direct words from the pastor, the pastoral visitor, or the hospital chaplain can remind people of a contact that began in the hospital and can continue beyond the hospital. *"Although I was sorry to see you so ill, it was a delight to visit and talk with you. Now that you are home, if there is anything that our parish can do for you, please call me. I would be happy to come by for a visit."* Warm words to a grieving family a few weeks after the event may help them see the parish church as an ongoing resource of faith.

Some groups might benefit by regular mailings—three or four times a year. These mailings might be more generic, such as a newsletter or information from the parish. Simple publish-ing programs that run on personal computers make putting a newsletter together pretty doable. (Even better, enlist people in the parish who produce newsletters professionally to help with this, and watch how they enjoy lending their talent.)

We know, to take another example, that a large percentage of parents who send their children to religious education or Catholic schools do not attend Mass. The variety of reasons for this absence from Mass might well surprise most active Catholics. Without judging or condescending, an attractive newsletter, focusing on the needs of parents and the opportunities for children at the parish, sent a few times a year can help parents feel connected to the parish. While this is no substitute for talking with parents and building up the personal relationships that might help them be more active in church, it can supplement all the parish's other efforts to reach them.

Another group that might benefit from a newsletter or set of brochures is that 35 percent of registered parishioners whom one never sees at the parish. These people are on our mailing list, but they seem to give no money, have no one in school or religious education, are involved in no organizations, and usually are unknown by anyone on the staff. We have their names; we just don't know who they are. Besides material the parish might produce, some third-party material might also be helpful for this group. Mailings, done respectfully but regularly, can put ideas and reinforce connections in this marginal group of Catholics. When they start thinking of returning to the Church, they have a set of notions that they can develop as part of their ongoing conversion.

The possibilities of further reaching those we know in a parish are endless once we start thinking of the mail as an opportunity to reach out and reinforce relationships, whether strong or weak, that people have with their parish.

## Mailing to Strangers

Beyond those whose names are known in some way to the parish, there are thousands of people who live in the environs of the average parish. Because surveys have shown that almost 45 percent of these neighbors do not have a regular church, this high percentage should very much command the attention of pastors and pastoral leaders. With this group, mail stands out as one way to show our parish's interest in them.

To be sure, this generalized mailing ranks as the "riskiest" kind of mailing in terms of tangible results. Mailing to "strangers" is riskiest because there is hardly any prior connection with the parish and, since these large mailings are done through third-class bulk permits, recipients are most likely to leave letters and fliers unopened and unread. But hard-and-fast presumptions of ineffectiveness should not be taken as the only word on the topic.

Stories abound of parishes that mailed to everyone in their own town where hundreds of people responded, either asking for information or wanting to register in the parishes. Sometimes the net comes up full. Again, in one downtown parish in a large Midwestern city, a parish mailing to some 6,000 residents of "new housing" produced dozens of responses and, even better, two people who joined the Catechumenate. Another parish on the East Coast mailed to residents of new high-rises, resulting in almost forty new registrations in the parish. Pastors who try this kind of bulk mailing will be surprised at how often, when they meet new people in the neighborhood, they will be readily recognized as "the one who sends things in the mail." While these mailings are risky in terms of results, results do come.

So parishes should not be afraid to consider how to use mail to reach these large anonymous groups. If costs are controlled and the mailing is designed right, a parish might reap surprising results. No mail that parishes send will create havoc in anyone's life; for every person who just tosses out a piece of parish mail, there will be others who will be gratified that a neighborhood church thought of them and sent something thoughtful along.

The process of preparing these kinds of large mailings to a more anonymous neighborhood group, or even to a more extensive potential audience, is analogous to the steps needed for any mailing:

- Prepare the database.
- Develop appropriate material.
- Send it out through the Postal Service.

However, each of these steps requires special attention because of the nature of this kind of mass mailing.

## Prepare the Database

It is one thing to go to the parish computer or the parish set of index cards, make a selection, reproduce the addresses and put them on envelopes; it is quite another thing to think of mailing to many thousands of people whose name and address one does not have. The first necessity for this kind of mass mailing will be acquiring a database of addresses.

The database needed will depend on the kind of mailing a parish is planning. In some areas, even in cities, it may be possible to develop a database by oneself, using parishioners or using a local reverse phone directory (which many local libraries carry). The process is as boring as anything imaginable, but, once developed, the parish has the use of that database as often as it wishes.

Certain parishes, for example, have been able to develop a reasonable database by simply having parishioners drive down the streets, note the addresses, and record them either manually or into a computer. If a parish is looking at a certain neighborhood, or can fairly clearly map out its own streets, then this method may be easier than it seems. One would develop a list of streets and, under each street, the number sequence.

For example, if Elm is a major street in a town, walking or driving down Elm might produce a set of numbers like 1, 3, 5, 7, 9, 11, 13, etc., up to 111; the numbers may skip and pick up again at 213 and proceed from there. It is a relatively easy thing to put these numbers and streets into a computer database. Under the category "name" in a database, put "Resident" or "Neighbors" or some generic designation. (Don't get too fancy because the Postal Service will work extra hard not to have to deliver third-class mail.) Obviously, the "city" and "zip" will, by and large, be the same for every address, so that the main task in constructing this kind of database lies in entering the number and the street name. Hundreds of these can be put into a computer in a short amount of time. Again, the work is boring but the list is usable again and again.

Even city dwellers can benefit from this way of generically developing a set of addresses because apartment houses often have a distinct sequence for the apartment numbers. In this case, since the number of the building will remain the same, one only has to vary the apartment number, typing 1A, 1B, 1C, etc., until all the apartments have been itemized. In cities where there are large high-rises, it might be possible to map buildings with hundreds of apartments without any great difficulty.

What if developing a database this way, on one's own, is too difficult or simply will not work for the particular kind of mailing a parish wishes to do? There is no reason to despair—many companies exist that would love to sell parishes the databases they seek, and can do so at a very reasonable expense.

Just about every set of yellow pages in the country has an entry under "Mailing Labels," "Mailing Lists," or "Mailing Houses." These yellow-page categories represent companies whose livelihood consists in providing specific kinds of mailing lists to various organizations that want to do bulk mail. Even more, they often would be happy to do the actual mailing itself, in some cases even the printing. Invariably, those who sell mailing lists are very accommodating; a simple phone call will uncover a friendly voice only too eager to develop the kind of list a parish wants.

The kind of desired list may vary from a certain section in

the parish, to the entire parish, to even an entire town or region. General things to keep in mind when buying lists:

- They are sold with "minimum numbers," so one needs a large enough population.
- Parts of zip code areas can be purchased if one knows the "carrier route" numbers of specific streets; the local post office can, if it wants to, provide carrier route information for the parish.
- They can be bought in duplicate, with the second, third or fourth duplicate list being less expensive than the original one.
- They can be produced on pressure-sensitive labels (if you have parishioners who will affix the labels) or in "Cheshire" format, usually four across, which professional mailers use when affixing labels.
- The more specific the list, the more expensive it will be.

Try to get the largest basic list possible to reach the minimum number of labels the parish has to purchase; it might be easier to overorder and simply not use some labels. Depending on the number involved, going with a mailing house using "Cheshire" labels saves a lot of work. (If the mailing house is also going to bring the mail to the post office, the amount of work saved will be all that greater.) But thousands of labels can be affixed by a team of six parishioners in a reasonable amount of time; this process is greatly helped if the parish provides nice hot coffee and some tasty goodies.

The "specificity" of the list calls for particular consideration because the natural instinct will be to purchase a list that has the "actual names and addresses" in an area that a parish wants to mail to. Salespersons will recommend these "actual name and address" lists. This recommendation, however, should be resisted as strongly as possible. In other words, parishes should almost invariably purchase "generic" mailings lists to "residents" rather than "specific" mailings lists with "Mr. and Mrs.

John Jones," etc., spelled out. Since this flies in the face of everything "personal" that is so important for evangelization, a little elaboration is needed.

The mailing lists with the "actual names" of people have several drawbacks. First of all, they are developed by reversing the telephone list and so, almost by definition, they exclude the addresses of everyone who does not have a telephone—in many cases, the very persons a parish might want to reach. Second, although these lists guarantee "92 percent accuracy," a parish has absolutely no way of knowing how many incorrect names are on the list. But the parish can be sure that 8 percent are probably inaccurate and that, in itself, is deadly. Third, even if names are accurate, they may be out-of-date in pastorally embarrassing ways. The list may know that "Mr. and Mrs. John Jones" live at 11 Elm Street, but it probably does not know that "Mr. Jones" died six months ago and "Mrs. Jones" is just furious that her parish, which celebrated her husband's funeral, is still writing to him. Multiply that by people who have experienced separation or divorce, children who have moved out, those who recently moved, and a range of other hidden factors, and one quickly gets the idea that it's just not worth paying the considerable extra amount to end up with blunders like this.

Anyone experienced in advertising or any parishioner skilled in bulk mailing can help a parish navigate through the various considerations in developing a bulk database.

## Develop Appropriate Material

Here, precisely because one is doing bulk mailing, the parish has to decide to strike the right kind of public and upbeat message.

"Public"—because the parish's message is going into the homes of many thousands of people who may have absolutely no knowledge of the parish. Therefore, those who develop the materials have to wear the "total stranger" hat and construct the mailing as if writing to people for whom nothing can be assumed. It makes little sense to talk about "eucharistic adoration" or "the St. John's Guild" or "Father Houlihy Hall" or any other instance of general or local "Catholic babble." Our lingo is our lingo; we cannot presume that strangers can make any sense of it. (On this score, most of what appears in the parish bulletin would also be inappropriate in a general mailing of this sort.)

"Upbeat"–because this kind of mailing represents a unique way to put forward the most positive and compelling features of your parish *as they might most be appreciated by the general searching public.* The aspects of your parish that touch the broadest and deepest strains of the human heart are exactly the ones that should be featured. Developing this kind of material takes special care because it runs against the kind of inner Catholic dialogue we are so used to carrying on. What is there about our parish—its worship, its mission, its people, its institutions—that would "grab" the interest of most of our neighbors? That's exactly what should be in the material that is being prepared.

Again, the exact shape of the material can be of several possible formats: letters, brochures, newsletters or even newspapers. Knowing their particular neighborhood, evangelization teams should be able to decide on the best format. Much of the design can be done "in-house" on a computer, but the more professional it looks, the more likely it will be read. In mailings of this magnitude, it is better to spend a bit more to look good than to save a few dollars and look foolish before many. Of course, photos and attractive type and layout are a must.

Developing the material need not be as costly as first imagined; with experience, parishes find ways to do things less expensively. Certain avenues should not be overlooked: bulletin companies often will print items on their "off days" at very reasonable rates; likewise, the diocesan newspaper might well print up "camera-ready" material if its presses would otherwise be sitting idle. Although one wants to be careful with this idea, one should not overlook local merchants who might want to sponsor a mailing. (Try not to have your material look too commercial or—even worse—if sponsored by several undertakers, macabre.)

## Putting It in the Post Office

This third part of bulk mailing would seem to the inexperienced to be the easiest phase. In reality, it is the most difficult phase and has caused parishes and other institutions tremendous frustration. Postal rules have changed a lot in recent years; more change can be expected as the Postal Service competes with other delivery systems and strives for greater efficiencies. Keeping up with the rule changes and following all the procedures properly can be a Herculean task.

Even so, many parishes that already regularly do bulk mailing will take this part of the mailing apostolate in stride. The contacts and systems that they employ with their regular bulk mailings will all fall into place when doing larger mailings. However, parishes that are innocent of bulk mailing will have something of a learning curve; once the procedure is mastered, each succeeding mailing will seem much easier.

What are the elements to consider in the mailing phase of this outreach? Review the following:

DOES THE PARISH HAVE PROPER POSTAL INDICIA?

A bulk mailing permit (a parish must apply for one or use another's permit under proper circumstances) is absolutely necessary. Most parishes have one. Often, however, they have let it lapse, but they can revive it by paying a certain fee. The permit must be affixed by stamp or printing if the indicia will be used in lieu of stamps or meter postage. Obviously, the stamping and printing must be correct. It is worth the effort to obtain such a permit—the amount saved on postage expenses will be quite substantial and can be used with other bulk mailings. The general mailing facility in your area will provide the current rules and examples as part of its service.

### IS THERE ENOUGH TIME?

Bulk mailing should never be used for time-critical mailings. Bulk mailing goes third-class, not first-class. One must plan for a time period potentially as long as three weeks, although it will rarely take that long. After one or two mailings, how long bulk mail actually takes in any particular neighborhood will become fairly clear. At any rate, one does not want to send fliers around about next week's spaghetti dinner unless the parish has a lot of freezer space for the leftover sauce.

### IS THE MATERIAL SORTED PROPERLY?

Bulk mail goes at a substantially reduced rate because the Postal Service is not doing most of the sorting. The mailer—in this case the parish—does. This sorting generally involves only the zip codes, but it can also involve carrier routes. The Postal Service will provide a detailed description of the way the sorting has to happen, the kinds of stickers that have to be attached to handfuls of mail banded together and to the tray or sack that holds the mail. Especially in big cities, the post office will be particularly unforgiving if the mail is sorted or bundled incorrectly.

### ARE THE MAILING PIECES FREE FROM SNAFUS?

One parish unknowingly bought what was represented as a "name-and-address list" with many thousands of labels. When it sent the mailing out, it had inadvertently printed under its return address the words "Address Correction Requested." The pastor was not happy when, every day, hundreds of letters were returned at a cost of fifty cents each!

Likewise, the return address of the parish should be printed correctly and the label affixed properly. Sometimes, in their zeal, volunteers will let a pile of letters go through without stamping the indicia or without slapping on the labels. Such mistakes add unnecessary costs to the mailing venture. Having one experienced person oversee the mailing will lessen the likelihood of errors arising from inexperience or haste.

## It Can Be Done

It should be obvious why parishes shy away from large-scale mailings; they are a lot of work and they involve skills and risks unusual in the lives of many parishes. The accumulation of the work and expense also leads parishes to presume a certain kind of response that may not be realistic. So the extra effort, combined with some disappointment, leads them to locate any large mailings far down on their list of priorities.

Such a skittishness, however, may not be warranted. With a little experience and patience, and at a cost less than might be imagined, a parish can actually start putting new ideas into the minds, and new intentions into the hearts, of a significant number of people who otherwise might not ever feel invited to any church, let alone the Catholic Church.

Mailing as apostolic outreach is not magic. It works along the same human dynamic as any other mailing. Like other mailings, it has to be attractive and it has to be consistent (one should do these mass mailings often enough to begin making an impression, perhaps three times a year). Like other mailings, however, it will have some effect, just as general mailings have come to touch, one way or another, our own lives.

It's not wise to predict the effect of a mailing ahead of time. Rather, with time, over several mailings, a parish will get a sense of being present in ways it was not before. In very subtle ways the fruits of mailing will start to appear: pastors will get phone calls, school principals will get inquiries, visitors will appear in church, extra donations will be made, and there will be a sense of energy that, while hard to put one's finger on, is undeniable.

Trusting in the power of this kind of communication, however, is more than reliance on the Postal Service or marketing gimmicks. If done in the proper spirit of faith and sharing, it will mostly be a reliance on the Spirit of God.

## HOME VISITATION

No apostolic outreach scares Catholics more than home visitation. One reason for this arises from the experience that Catholics have of those groups that regularly do home visitation—Jehovah's Witnesses, for example. Saturday after Saturday the handful of home visitors from this group will knock on doors, sometimes with a persistence that borders on discourtesy. Catholics, and the population in general, just do not like being visited this way.

The other reason comes from the ignorance of Catholics: so few of them have ever visited the homes of others on behalf of their parish that the very idea grotesquely enlarges itself in the vacuum of Catholic imagination into some terrible monster. "What will happen if I knock on doors?" Catholics think; they proceed to answer their question with the most frightful images their minds can produce.

Just like every other evangelization strategy, home visitation has its distinct advantages and disadvantages. The tragedy is that, because home visitation has become something of a corrupted image in today's isolated society, parishes cannot easily grasp the particular advantages to home visitation. They get stumped on the disadvantages.

There are two main disadvantages in visiting homes: (1) it is very labor-intensive work, and (2) home visiting has become very "out of fashion" in modern life, particularly in the suburbs. There are ways, however, to lessen the intensity of the labor if parishes will take a long-range view of home visitation.

And when it is done with respect, most Catholics who engage in home visitation find it to be a positive and affirming activity.

Against these disadvantages, which we will have to look at again in the pages ahead, there are very clear advantages to home visitation: (1) it allows us to meet people whom we should be meeting, particularly those who have no church for all practical purposes as well as those who have ceased being active in their Catholic faith; (2) it puts a human face onto the often overly institutional face of today's parishes; and (3) it both portrays and instills a distinct vitality in the parish community.

## Visitation Possibilities

Because home visitation is labor intensive, when parishes engage in it, usually only a small group of dedicated people will be willing to undertake this activity as a steady diet. Parishes have had, and still have, followers of the Legion of Mary, many of whom still put home visitation on the top of their agenda. Likewise, some evangelization committees have converted themselves primarily into home visitation committees. In both these cases, what usually happens is that a small handful of people survive in this ministry—and everyone else in the parish decides that it's not for them.

A general rule about home visitation can be stated: if a group *exclusively* visits homes, it will probably be a small group. Chances are excellent, too, that this group will feel a bit isolated from most of the other activity in the parish ("We meet people when we visit, but it's hard to know what to do with them"). It may plug into the pastor's office easily, but the other levels of parish organization will seem more remote or even irrelevant.

Some of this can be addressed by designing home visitation as an *episodic* thing: particular periods of the year when parishioners are invited to visit a specific range of homes with a particular purpose. If parishes conceive home visitation this way, they will find a larger group of Catholics who are willing to "give a few hours" in a month or six weeks to visiting others. When these Catholics feel positive about their home visitation, they will be willing to engage in the activity on a regular basis. Evangelization leaders will be surprised at how many Catholics find this kind of limited, defined home visitation a very positive thing to do.

Parishes, in designing home visitation efforts, need to consider how to interconnect short-term and long-term strategies. Settling only for long-term strategies, like "visiting every home in our parish," will significantly limit some of the possibilities of visitation, even though it will gain the parish a small corps of dedicated home visitors.

## Kinds of Visits

Home visitation divides itself into three general kinds of visits: (1) the census visit, (2) the social visit and (3) the witness visit. For reasons that will become clear when we talk about the "grammar" of home visitation, none of these kinds of visits can be strictly distinguished from the others. A visit will take on its own life and meaning as Catholics engage in the effort. However, each of these types has particular considerations.

*The Census Visit.* Pastors will sometimes call for the parish to undertake a census of the parish. This can mean two things: either everyone in the parish is going to be visited (this is called more properly *canvassing*) or only the Catholics on record will be visited so that their census information can be updated.

Catholics respond well to the idea of a census because it seems like something that parishes have always done or need to do periodically. Depending on the kind of census that is being taken, the approach of the home visit will be very different. Visiting people that the parish "knows" because it has information already (name, address, family size, etc.) is very different from visiting people whom the parish does not clearly know. Walking up to a door with a census card that already has information on it feels very unlike walking up to a door when the visitors have no idea who is behind the door.

Here are important considerations that pastors and pastoral leaders have to keep in mind in designing this kind of visit:

- Will the visit be to everyone, or will it be a revision of census data we already have?
- What are the questions that are being asked on the census form and why?
- Who will enter the census data, and who will be responsible to keep it up-to-date?
- What is the pastoral worth of standing before nonparishioners with strange-looking forms asking some personal questions?

Taking a census cannot happen successfully unless these basic questions are answered. Pastors can get some guidance from their chancery offices, which often have a diocesan "census card" and may even have software for entering data.

*The Social Visit.* This kind of visitation falls into the "neighbor" category of modern life: parishioners, as neighbors, visit others in their neighborhood so as to get to know them and to make themselves known.

This kind of visit also is attractive to Catholics because they realize that their parish is unknown to many people in the neighborhood; they also know that neighborhoods change with a great deal of frequency today because of the high mobility of society. So it makes some basic human sense to try to meet new people and introduce the resources of the parish to them.

The social visit can be designed to visit everyone, to visit a particular sector of the parish (e.g., seniors, or parents of grade-school-age children), or a particular area (e.g., a newly developed area or an older area that has experienced change). The social visit also provides a great deal of flexibility in how a visit might actually evolve.

The social visit raises its own set of questions:

- Why are *these* particular people being visited and not others in the parish?
- What is the overall purpose of the visit? Is this clear to the visitors?
- How will follow-up, if there is any, happen?
- Does this visit have enough substance to it to be worth the time and effort?

Answering these and other questions that will arise are important parts of designing a home visit.

*The Witness Visit.* This kind of home visit has a specific religious design to it. Catholics go forth witnessing to their faith and seek some kind of response from those who are visited. Some Catholic groups have designed home visiting quite clearly based on Protestant evangelical models, which, almost by definition, are witness visits.

In theory a witness visit makes a lot of sense for Protestant evangelicals, whose theology does not constrain them to bring people to church or sacraments or community. In a purely evangelical Protestant construct, people can "find Jesus" and "be saved" right on their doorstep. Catholics, who understand evangelization in the broader patterns of church and community, cannot leave people on their doorstep.

Even so, the idea of Catholics witnessing to faith has a tremendous power to it, primarily because Catholics seem so rarely to be doing this. For exactly this same reason, however, Catholics will probably be most reluctant to be doing this kind of home visitation. If they can understand a census and if they can make sense of a social visit, the idea of strangers witnessing their faith to other strangers in a doorway seems a particularly alien notion in today's society. A lot of work has to go into selling this idea.

Some considerations for parishes who wish to undertake this kind of visitation are:

- How will Catholic witness be formulated so that a general public can readily understand it?
- How does one get both Catholics and strangers comfortable with this kind of visit today?
- What is one seeking from this kind of visit? Can the objectives be clarified?
- What will follow-up mean, and who will do it?
- To what ongoing parish activities or ministries will people be referred?

Unless this kind of home visit is very carefully designed and thought out, it will be almost impossible for Catholics to engage in it. If it can be designed and carried out credibly in a particular locale, it will be a very powerful tool for reaching people in faith.

## Listening

Catholics who have experience with home visitation know that, in some basic way, the particular kind of visit may be irrelevant because people will either open up and talk with the visitors or they will not.

The object of every visit is **just this kind of dialogue.** Whether taking the census, socially dropping in or making a kind of faith statement, all of this truly is seed that is being sown.

The key to the visit is the response that people make to the visitors. Visitors must be sensitive enough to be able to know what others are asking when the visit starts to go a little deeper, when others are reaching out for some kind of help, enlightenment or direction.

Because we never know who is on the other side of the door when we knock (even if we have their name and address), we never know how the Spirit of God has been working in their lives. Neither can we know what exactly will be evoked from the hearts of others when believers come knocking on their doors.

Home visitors need to be especially sensitive to the signs that something is happening in the lives of people and the home visit has stumbled upon that. Signals to look for are:

- when one is invited into the home
- when one is offered refreshments
- when one asks for more information about the parish or a particular program
- when one says things like, "I'm so glad you came," or, "I've been thinking about something"
- when people evince a high level of emotion at the visit
- when people ask the visitors to drop by again
- when people express particular needs for prayer

These and similar reactions can happen no matter what kind of home visit is undertaken. The fruit of the visit will be precisely here, in the power it has to evoke deeper religious issues and bring them out into the open.

Visitors need to be sensitive to these signals and also to know what to do in response to the appearance of this kind of deeper agenda.

### The Grammar of Home Visiting

The word *grammar* refers to various regularities and connections made in language. Home visiting has regular patterns and connections that govern the whole exercise of strangers visiting the door of another. By noticing some of these patterns, it will be possible to design home-visiting ventures with greater realism and prospects of greater success. Again, as in all these efforts, parishes will be most frustrated if they do not use a particular tool for exactly what it can accomplish. Expecting home-cooked meals from deli meats will inevitably disappoint.

Consider the following patterns and regularities in the process of home visiting.

### THE HOME VISIT IS GOVERNED BY THE "NEED TO PLEASE."

So rare is it in contemporary society (as opposed to only a generation ago) for people to knock on the doors of others (or ring their doorbells), the very sound of someone at the door fills the dweller with intimations of fear. "Who could be at the door? What time is it? I'm not expecting anyone. I haven't heard my doorbell ring since I moved in. What could they want? Am I ready to receive someone?"

Likewise the visitor is going through his or her set of apprehensions. "Who is on the other side? Am I disturbing them? Will they be friendly or indifferent or angry? What am I going to say? What will they think of me? Can they see how nervous I am?"

As a result of these absolutely normal and predictable fears, there arises a "need to please," a need for people to say and do the kinds of courteous and civil things to alleviate the tension without it costing either party too much. Argument, disagreement, discord and tension will be avoided at any cost because, in that kind of fume-filled nervous encounter, who knows what kind of explosion might be set off?

The upshot of this comes down to the tendency of each party to say agreeable things that they somewhat mean. If asked a question, someone will answer "yes" if that is where the drift of the question leads. "Are there believers in this house?" Chances are very excellent that a "yes" will be said because what would a "no" lead to?

This in no way diminishes the value of a visit; it's just one of the "grammatical" rules that affect the exchange.

### THE ONE BEING VISITED CONTROLS THE VISIT.

This is so obvious, a critic might well wonder why it is being stated at all. Yet the very moxie that it takes to visit the homes of strangers in today's society gives the visitor an entirely different sense.

The visitor often believes that such an imposition is being created by the visit that this alone is the dominant feeling or affect of the visit. The private space of another is being transgressed by people at the door. How does this come across? "We are invading the house of another" might well be one way to read the situation. "We are disrupting the lives of other people." As a result, visitors can implicitly have a false sense of intrusion or, even worse, aggression, as they approach someone's door.

With this in mind, it is important for the visitors to be reminded that the whole visit is, and will remain, under the control of the persons in the house. They have choices at every step: to pay attention to a doorbell, to open a door, to open a door just a crack or wide, to smile or not, to pursue the conversation or not, to ask the visitors to please leave, to come back some other time or never to approach the doorway again.

Every hint of manipulation should be avoided in home visiting, and no visit should be designed with deceptive or compromising techniques to get into the door. People must be free to respond as they wish. Yet visitors must not assume that this freedom has been taken away simply by the act of knocking on a door.

THE VISITORS CONTRIBUTE TO THE DYNAMICS OF
THE VISIT BY THEIR AFFECT.

Because of the cautious nature of appearing at someone's doorway today, visitors need to be constantly aware of the importance of the way they "set up" a home visit. This usually comes down, apart from the personalities of the visitors, to the initial introduction and statement of the purpose of the visit.

While the people inside the household will control the ultimate dynamics of the visit, those at the doorway contribute to those dynamics by their personal affect. The body language, the facial gestures, the mode of speaking, the subtle tones that signal an inner attitude—these have powerful impact on the way a visit will work out.

Visitors have to be sure never to put people on the defensive, never to give people the feeling that they are being judged or are part of some kind of inquisition, never to feel bowled over by the nature of the initial presentation, and never to feel that they said more than they intended and will regret it later.

If visitors give an officious impression that they are personal ambassadors of the local archbishop and are present on some kind of formal business (this is not so implausible), the encounter will be shaped a certain way. If they give the impression that they are personal ambassadors of Jesus and come with the people and good wishes with which he sent his disciples forth (see Lk 10:5 ff.), then an entirely different kind of encounter will be shaped.

While the whole visit is not determined by the visitors, it will be influenced by them.

WHEN THE VISIT IS OVER, ITS BASIC PURPOSE HAS BEEN ACCOMPLISHED.

Because of the "need to please," both visitors and those being visited will say gracious and wonderful things. However, once the visit ends, the whole power of the event significantly decreases and those inside the household return very quickly to their own "space."

What this means in practical terms is that although certain outcomes may be part of the objectives of a visit, these will not invariably follow. Nor should visitors be distracted by these possible outcomes. The truth is this: the power of the visit will reside in the visit itself. What happens during the visit occurs in the dynamics between human beings as those dynamics are touched by the power of the Spirit of Christ. That, in itself, represents a wonderful event in the Kingdom of God. Visitors should not be distracted from the wonder of that event in itself.

Often visitors, or their pastors, will be looking for all kinds of other outcomes from the visit. Because the doorway is a completely different world from any other in today's society, the spillover from a home visit to actual behaviors beyond the visit may not be visible. Those inside the household may have said things or responded a certain way; they may also have forgotten, not too long after the visit ends, what they said or promised.

This hardly means the visit was a waste of time. It means that the impact of the visit will be primarily during the visit itself. Certainly people may want follow-up and invite the visitors to call or visit again. Certainly people may think about their attitude toward Christ, toward the Church or toward their religious behavior. Certainly they may feel a greater identity with their children's religious education teacher or scout master. But the primary impact will be the moment of grace that happens when people look into one another's faces with faith and trust.

These four factors have a major impact on the possibilities and limits of home visiting. When parishes design home visits, they need to bear these "grammar rules" in mind, both to exploit the possibilities and to escape some potential disillusionment.

### "Designing a Visit"

In view of the various factors involved in home visitation that have been reviewed in the preceding sections, pastoral teams can begin designing home visitation ministries with a greater sense of the framework and the pitfalls of home visiting. Pastoral teams may find the following principles helpful as they design these home visits.

### 1. Every home visit needs to be designed from scratch.

No two visits are the same. Every home visit should be designed carefully, after considering three basic components:

- Who is being visited?
- Who is doing the visiting?
- What is the purpose?

Only a thorough grasp of these three basic components will provide the apostolic context for designing what a home visit will look like. Groups like the Legion of Mary are successful in the kind of home visiting they do because they have developed a basic design and stick with it.

Evangelization teams will have to carefully envision who is being visited (their age, lifestyle, obligations, needs, etc.), and who is going to do the visit (seniors, young adults, parents, a particular organization in the parish, etc.). Carefully trying to imagine the dynamics of these two groups, along with a very clear sense of what the parish hopes to accomplish from the visit, will help the parish to design a fruitful visit.

## 2. Only teams should do home visiting.

Visitors should never go out by themselves; to do so, in today's society, can put them at personal physical and legal risk. At the same time, probably no more than two people should ever approach someone's door. People do not want the feeling that they are being "ganged up on." Teams of two, which go back to Jesus, still make the most sense today.

Teams should be composed of two people for whom visiting is proper. Bringing children along should be prohibited out of hand; having adolescents visit probably can be justified only if they are visiting other adolescents. Catholics should not even seem like they are exploiting their children or youth, whatever practical or good intentions they might have.

## 3. The geographical scope of the visit should be carefully planned.

Before a visit can happen, the area needs to be mapped and the number of needed visitors has to be calculated. Pastoral and evangelization teams have to carefully draw the geographical scope of the home visitation, taking into account the probable limits of the home visitors. What is the point of saying, "We will visit every home," if there will never be enough volunteers found in a parish to accomplish this? Similarly, home visitors have a right to get some sense of what is being asked of them, whether they will be expected to visit for a long period of time or for some short, definable length of time.

It is unrealistic to assign more than twenty to thirty homes to a team for any one visiting session. One can presume that half the homes will not respond and that, of the ones that respond, some good conversation will occur in one out of three of those. So a team, in a two-to-three-hour visiting session, can expect to get responses from ten homes and get good conversations in about three of them, with one of them taking up a good amount of time.

With this kind of average experience, planning teams can figure out how many houses to include in the general scope of the visitation and also decide how many visiting sessions each team of two visitors will be asked to do.

### 4. "Script" the visit.

Part of designing a visit is "scripting it," not in the sense of having stilted visitors with memorized lines, but in the sense of giving the visitors and those being visited a good chance of knowing what the visit is for and a sense of ease in accomplishing it.

A "script" may well include the following items:

- introductions
- a statement of whom the visitors represent
- a statement of the purpose of the visit
- an opening question and any follow-up questions
- sharing information and any articles that might be part of the visit

- asking if there are any particular needs the parish or visitors might attend to
- offering to pray for particular needs (and even praying as part of the visit)
- stating any follow-up commitments
- farewells

Much thought must go into the statement of the purpose of the visit and the opening question. If people are not clear why someone is at their front door, or if the opening question makes people feel awkward, the visit has a harder chance of being successful.

These "scripts" should be roughed out with various foreseen responses so that visitors have some overall sense of how a visit might proceed. For example, if the opening question is, "We are looking for Catholics who live in our area; are there any baptized Catholics who are part of your household?" a script might anticipate a "yes" and a "no" as well as an "I'm not sure."

Part of planning a visit will be to think about including any material or artifacts that might be appropriate for a visit. Many parishes, for example, have basements full of booklets done for one or another anniversary. If one is visiting parishioners, giving one of these books as a visiting gift might be a great gesture. Let the planning team be creative in designing a pastoral visit that speaks of the warmth of the parish community.

## 5. Have visitors prepare by role-playing.

Visitors can get some sense of how the home visits may go through some realistic role-playing. This can be done only after the visit is designed and a "script" is prepared. Part of the training of visitors should concentrate on their being at ease with the visit as it is envisioned. Role-playing, with various parishioners playing both the visitor and the one being visited, will put people at ease (and invariably also produce some hilarious moments). This all helps parishioners deal with the inevitable tensions that are part of doing this ministry.

## 6. Prepare items for the home visit.

Visitors should be equipped with certain resources to make the visit successful. Those who are planning the home visitation might use the following checklist to help plan the visit:

- identification cards or badges for the visitors
- an introductory letter
- maps of the area with the sequence of house numbers
- names and addresses of parishioners who live in the area to be visited
- basic material about the parish and/or neighborhood; this might well include basic material about other churches and houses of worship in the area
- any gift items the visitors will bring (calendars, baked goods, magnetic mementos of the parish, anniversary booklets, etc.)
- a notebook for any follow-up actions

Not all these items will be needed for every visit, but these and items like them will be needed as the shape of the visit comes into focus.

It is a very good idea to send a "general" letter to the homes that will be visited. Never tell people exactly what time the visitors will arrive; unless the parish is in an exceptional area where people swoon with neighborliness, more than likely such exact notification will be an opportunity for people *not* to be home. But a "general" letter that explains the purpose of the visit, explains that sometime in the next few weeks two visitors will be coming from the parish, and acknowledges ahead of time the welcome they will receive, can be a great preparation for the home visit. Part of the introductions that make up the visit can allude to the letter: "Did you receive the letter our pastor sent?"

## 7. Set up the prayerful context of the visit.

Home visiting will have much more impact if the whole parish is joined in prayer for the visitors. This prayer should be done when the congregation gathers for Mass on Sunday and also throughout the week. Seniors, shut-ins and children can participate in the visit by their personal prayer.

The visitors themselves should be infused with a spirit of prayer. They should meditate on Lk 10: 1–10 and see themselves as an extension of the seventy-two that Jesus sent out to prepare for his visit and announce the Kingdom. Visitors should spend time prior to the home visit praying for its success. Likewise, before they set out in the car or on foot, they should pray together for the grace that will accompany their visit and pray in gratitude when the visiting session ends.

## 8. Debrief the visitors and make appropriate reports.

Those who visit homes are undergoing powerful experiences. They need, and deserve, a forum to help them understand what has been accomplished through their visiting. Part of the time one asks of visitors should include an hour or so for them to report what happened on the visit, bringing up any episodes that confused them, and elaborating on events that excited and consoled them.

If these debriefing sessions are not held, visitors will not be inclined to visit homes again. However, if these modern disciples of Christ are allowed to express their feelings and observations, they will feel empowered to appreciate what God did through them and to do the visiting again in the future.

Reports of the visit should also be prepared for the pastor and pastoral council, with some summary given in the bulletin. These reports will invariably be more impressive than anyone imagined in the beginning and will be a great incentive for the parish to continue its outreach in a variety of forms.

## Let's Visit in the Lord's Name

Home visiting carries tremendous power. It flows from the outreach begun in God, who, in the words of Zachariah's canticle, "has visited his people" (Lk 1:67); it has flowed throughout history through divine revelation and, most pressingly, in the person of his Son, Jesus Christ.

The whole New Testament is a narrative of what happens when people meet others in Christ. Apostles are "sent" to gather people together; they meet in homes, homes that become the first churches of the followers of Jesus. Jesus explicitly sends his apostles and disciples forth during his earthly ministry; his Spirit empowers his disciples after Easter to go forth with the message of his resurrection, of his Spirit and of the community of love that he has begun as the initial stage of his Kingdom.

Many of these sending and gathering dynamics that are implicit in the Christian faith are invisible dynamics today because Catholics have gotten into a routine that revolves almost entirely around parish and "going to church." The sending and gathering that lie at the heart of Christianity become obscured and lose their evangelical power.

Home visiting, and other outreach strategies envisioned in Goal II of the U.S. bishops' *Go and Make Disciples,* can go a long way to helping the contemporary Church recover the evangelizing dynamics without which it cannot thrive.

## Reflection: Reaching Out

*He invited me and I was afraid.*

*I was only a simple fisherman, used to getting up early, staying up late, searching the lake endlessly for signs of fish. I got used to the strain and struggle of pulling in the net, the excitement and fatigue fused together. I got used to the quiet, peaceful monotony of sewing the torn net.*

*Then he invited me. And everything has been different since then.*

*He invited me to follow, along with my brother and friends, as we wandered the roads in Galilee. He astonished us by what he did. His teaching kept me, and the crowds around me, spellbound.*

*Then he shocked me. Because he invited me to go out myself, with my brother, to announce his Kingdom in his name. To even bring his Kingdom by the exchange of peace, by the prayers we'd say, by the healings we would sometimes do.*

*I never thought I could do it. I stayed up all night worrying about what would happen. He had to encourage me. He reminded me that it was the hearts of people I now was fishing for.*

*I went, on his invitation. I spoke his word to others. I acted as he acted. I shared what Jesus gave me to share, even to consoling, to freeing people from evil, to bringing God's healing to the broken.*

*He invited me. I was afraid, but after I said "yes," I began to realize what Jesus was all about. The invitation.*

# Chapter 4

---

# EVANGELIZATION TEAMS

Throughout this little manual we've mentioned "evangelization teams" with some frequency. This, however, does not mean that the existence of an evangelization team in the parish is *presumed.* In fact, the opposite is probably the case.

Most parishes still have not formed an evangelization team, or if they have formed one, it may well be crippled in its operation.

What's the problem? It seems to come from two distinct sources. First, parishes often think that they do not need an evangelization team since "everyone is doing evangelization." Second, once evangelization teams are formed, they are often left isolated, that is, unconnected in any real way to the heart of the parish. We should look just a bit more carefully at each of these reasons because they contain assumptions or oversights that need to be addressed.

### Everyone Does Evangelization

The downside of Pope Paul VI's insistence that evangelization is the basic ministry of the Church, and that all the baptized are evangelizers, usually shows itself in a rather widespread impression: "Everything we do is evangelization." While this may be true, it hardly means the parish is doing everything it should be doing.

It clearly is true that everything a parish does is evangelization and every ministry in some way relates to the broad vision of evangelization. That, however, is hardly a recipe for parishes to do exactly what they have been doing and nothing more, as if they were absolved from any further challenge or growth. In fact, if the vision of evangelization has caught on in a parish, it has to show itself in both deeper and broader patterns of ministry. The parish's pursuit of the Word of God in a life of discipleship will create a permanent desire to enter more deeply into the Spirit of God. Likewise, the parish's pursuit of the fullness of the Kingdom will instill a permanent will to extend the message of the Good News to others who have not yet heard it.

Evangelization certainly is not merely a question of doing "more," as if frenetic activity justified anything other than our modern obsessive way of life. But evangelization, in its depth and breadth, evokes from the parish the fuller inward and outward dimensions of its own life.

Certain of those dimensions are not easily accepted by modern parish communities. Any honest survey of the modern parish, and the ordinary life of modern Catholics, will show that Catholic life is weakest in the areas that this handbook emphasizes—in the inviting, welcoming and proclaiming dimensions of faith. Even if these are present in a parish, they often exist so subtly and so without energy that many parishioners themselves do not have awareness of them.

"Everyone does evangelization." Indeed; but who does the outreach? Who thinks about who *isn't* coming to church and why? Who explores the parish's reach beyond its own membership, particularly to those who are most without voice or least likely to feel welcomed by the parish? Who raises the consciousness of the parish about its own missionary core? Who articulates the silent voice of the inactive Catholic, the angry Catholic, the marginalized Catholic?

Parishes need evangelization teams precisely to keep this *outward* thrust of their life on target and clearly visible. These teams also, among all the organizations and ministries of the parish, are most likely to develop the ministerial activities needed to invite those "others" whom the Spirit of God would touch.

*Go and Make Disciples* called for an evangelization team in every parish (and one in every diocese too). Some dioceses have gone a long way toward making this notion real; others use evangelization language but betray few clear evangelizing actions and even less evangelizing planning.

As long as evangelization teams, or their equivalent, are not part of our Catholic landscape, a large part of the power of evangelization will be lost to our churches.

## *Isolated Teams*

Often parishes set up evangelization teams. But six months or a year later, the members of the team find themselves floundering and confused, unable to find energy or direction.

"Isolation" is the most likely reason for this sense that "the wind has gone out of our sails" and "we don't know where we are going." Pastors can address the issue of isolation and help rescue many frustrated Catholic evangelizers.

"Isolation" refers to the organizational configuration by which an evangelization team feels unconnected in any real way to the key ministerial dimension of a parish. They meet. They say and feel things. They may even decide to do things. But it feels like it's all happening in a vacuum.

When they want to get something in the bulletin, it's a strain. When they want to use a facility, it's a hassle. When they want to meet with the pastor, he's busy or "he'll stop by at the meeting"—and does so only for a few of the briefest moments.

It's almost like evangelization teams are alien creatures

that somehow landed in a parish; the parish's way of coping with these aliens is to pretend they are not there, that they do not exist.

Pastors and parishes do not intend this sense of isolation. It has little to do with goodwill or even perceived needs—parishes have the goodwill and clearly see the needs. Rather, it is mostly a structural problem in the parish's organization. It can, therefore, be solved by some clearer structural thinking on the part of the pastor and the pastoral leadership.

In establishing an evangelization team, the parish must decide how the team will relate to the parish as a whole or to the other ministries of the parish. A team can, for the most part, relate in four ways:

1. under the pastoral council
2. under the pastor
3. under a pastoral associate
4. on its own

Of these four alternatives, only the first works best because all the other possibilities have built-in weaknesses. If the team understands itself as a committee of the pastor or a committee of a pastoral associate, its access to the main planning and life of the parish will be only through that person. It can then begin to feel that it has no standing on its own. Even worse, the pastor or pastoral associate can forget to link the evangelization team to other ministries; in this way, they feel like they are left "hanging." Evangelization teams sometimes have the horrible feeling that they do not even relate to a pastoral staff person; they are left on their own. This is a sure way to demoralize an evangelization team. They feel that they speak to no one and that their plans are intrusions on everything else the parish is doing.

Pastors, however, can rectify these feelings of being out in "left field" by the way they structure the evangelization team and have it relate to other entities in the parish. Having the evangelization team relate to the pastoral council, as either a standing committee or a reporting committee, accomplishes two things: (1) it opens communication between the team and the council so that basic information is being shared, and (2) it brings an evangelization awareness to the council that will begin to infuse all its thinking.

Often parishioners want to get involved in evangelization and feel they cannot convince their pastor. That is tragic. More tragic still, however, is a pastor who sees the need for an evangelization team but fails to support it and thereby isolates it. In the one case, no promises were made; in the other, promises were made and then compromised.

## Team Direction

Evangelization teams have meetings. Those meetings form the precious moments that give the team direction and energy. The leadership on these teams, therefore, must have some sense of how to conduct a meeting and how to view the committee's work in the overall plan of the parish.

We have all almost died at meetings, so boring and pointless did they seem. Likewise, we've all had our committee work lose perspective and even its basic orientation because vision was not supplied or some particular agenda started replacing the evangelization agenda that should be the heart of the committee's work.

At any price, these two pitfalls should be avoided.

### CONDUCTING A MEETING

Evangelization teams will have successful (if not always exciting) meetings if some consideration is given to planning the meeting and, as important, the committee actually follows the plan. Here are some things to consider:

- Begin on time.
- Begin with prayer and some time for sharing, preferably on a Scripture selection.

- Publish and stick to an agenda.
- Help the committee maintain a pleasant and faith-filled disposition in its work.
- Emphasize collaboration.
- Make sure the agenda items are clear and someone is ready to present or address each item.
- Define the tasks that result from the meeting.
- Assign responsibility for carrying out the tasks.
- Assign the communicating that has to happen as a result of the meeting (i.e., who talks to the pastor, the liturgists, and any others affected by the committee's deliberations; who writes what letters; what goes in the bulletin; etc.).
- Do not let issues get talked to death.
- Make sure everyone has the say she or he wants.
- Do not let anyone monopolize the meeting.
- Bring the issues that are ready forward to resolution and decision; let the issues that need more time wait until the group is ready.
- Define clearly what is resolved and what is not resolved.
- Have a basic idea of how long the meetings will go.
- Set the time and place for the next meeting.
- Stick to the schedule and end on time.

An evangelization team that senses that its work is going somewhere cannot help but be responsive and energetic when it meets. This enthusiasm will also spread beyond itself.

Not infrequently, when a parish initiates an evangelization team and that team has energy to produce results, many of the other ministries and organizations of the parish will say, "Gee, why can't we be like the evangelization team?" The energy is contagious.

However, the Holy Spirit cannot produce this kind of enthusiasm and direction if the committee will not lay the basis for the Spirit's work by attending to what is necessary to bring people together, giving them a voice, helping that voice be shaped toward a resolution and then following up that resolution with assignments to make the decisions take on pastoral shape.

## KEEPING AN ORIENTATION

Evangelization teams, because they are not presently seen as integral to a parish (like catechetical teams, for example), always run the risk of losing their orientation. As part of the phenomenon of these teams becoming isolated, they seem to float apart from the central dynamics of a parish, attempt a variety of things haphazardly, and quickly get the sense that the parish doesn't quite know what to do with them.

Evangelization team leadership has the responsibility of helping the team and the parish interpret the effect of the evangelization committee in terms of the team's own goals and the overall goals of the parish.

This can sound a lot more "officious" than it actually is: we are not dealing here with high-level organizational maneuvers but rather with the simple task of helping the pertinent people know where everyone else is. Leadership makes this happen by communicating and by regularly helping the team review where it has been and where it is going.

Every effective team will engage in activities that spring from the vision and needs of the parish; returning to that vision and reviewing those needs helps root the activities of a team into the kind of larger framework that gives it orientation and grounding. Every evangelization team will, at some point, begin to ask itself, "Why did we begin this ministry? Why did we embark on this project?" This is a natural function of a group's self-guidance. Unless the team can understand why its particular efforts began and how they relate to the parish, it will become discouraged and exhausted.

In terms of its orientation within the parish, the evangelization team should:

- Know the vision of the parish (its mission statement).
- Conduct a pastoral assessment of the parish.
- Check that pastoral assessment with the parish's leadership (pastor, staff, pastoral council and perhaps the finance council).
- Report regularly to the leadership of the parish.
- Appropriately report to the whole parish through the bulletin or newsletter.
- Continue to check the team's efforts against the articulated mission of the parish.
- Review its efforts in an annual report (which it can give to the pastor).

Such efforts will be rewarded by an evangelization team that feels connected to the parish and understands the contribution it is making to the parish. Likewise, the parish will benefit by coming to understand all its efforts as more clearly evangelizing. Orienting the committee to the parish, in other words, helps everyone.

In terms of helping the committee keep its own orientation in line with its apostolic activities, leadership can keep the team on focus by:

- keeping the results of a pastoral assessment of the parish fresh
- helping the team select a few doable goals in terms of the parish's needs
- relating the activities of the team to *Go and Make Disciples* or the local diocese's evangelization plan
- regularly reviewing how the committee selected certain goals and the needs out of which they sprang
- making sure that members responsible for certain tasks accomplish them and report to the team

- developing the environment of prayer and religious celebration that reinforces the evangelizing imperative of the
  parish

Modern Americans like to look at charts and graphs to get a
whole perspective on such issues as their mutual fund portfo-
lios or the success of their dieting. Evangelization activities cannot be easily graphed and charted; however, the visioning
activities suggested here will go a long way toward surrounding
the committee with the sense that it is on track and connected.

## Pastoral Assessment

Evangelization teams face a problem similar to an author's:
when looking at a blank page, they may not know "where to
start." They have something akin to "writer's block." We can
call it "Gospel block."

The Good News, and our desire to deepen it in our lives and
spread it to others, can seem such an overwhelming task that it
just stuns parishes and evangelization teams into inactivity.
They don't know where to begin. Everything they think about
seems so vast and almost impossible.

Doing a pastoral assessment of the parish helps overcome
this "Gospel block." Again, this concept does not have to have
the weight of some corporate-executive study. It simply means
that a team looks at the parish in terms of the meaning and
goals of evangelization. On the basis of that look, it identifies
certain clear needs. With those needs in mind, the team
decides which ones the parish can and should tackle. This
brings some clarity to "where we should begin." It also will
give the rationale for all the activity that comes from a committee and keep it from mistaking trees for forests (and, more dan-
gerously, mistaking forests for trees).

*Go and Make Disciples,* the U.S. bishops' plan and strategy
for evangelization in the United States, was not written to be an

assessment tool, but its three goals, each elaborated with a succession of objectives and strategies, can well serve as a starting point for the pastoral assessment of the parish. It will force a team to look at the parish's own self-renewal, at its outreach to the unchurched and inactive, and at its impact on its surrounding world. Under each of these general goals, a range of possible objectives provides some concrete picture of how evangelizing (or not) a parish is.

These pastoral assessments obviously should not be conducted in a vacuum. The team should invite liturgists, catechists, staff persons and other appropriate ministries in the parish to help establish its own particular goals.

## A Great Resource

Parishes that establish and support evangelization teams will find them an enormous resource for all the efforts of the parish.

The team's work will supplement and intensify the effect of the efforts of other ministries in the parish (e.g., the adult Catechumenate, catechesis, the social justice committee) as well as provide a phalanx of important evangelizing efforts that simply fall through the cracks or, more probably, are not even recognized (e.g., developing ministries for inactive Catholics).

Organized properly, these teams will not at all be a hindrance to the work of the parish. Rather, they will be important assets, and as they mature, they will become essential assets.

They will be the way a parish keeps the demands of evangelization honestly and clearly before its eyes. They will also be a spearhead for organizing and accomplishing a significant part of that agenda. They will provide for the parish what key passages in the New Testament provide for our Catholic self-understanding, passages like the sending of the Twelve Apostles (Mk 6:7 ff.), the sending of the seventy-two disciples (Lk 10:1 ff.), the great mandate at the end of Matthew's Gospel

(Mt 28:10 ff.), the miraculous catch of fish (Jn 21:1 ff.), Peter's kerygmatic preaching (e.g., Acts 3:12 ff.), Paul's passionate involvement with his newly founded communities (Phil 1:3 ff.), even the exultant vision of Revelation as the heavenly Jerusalem finally is revealed in the glory of Christ's Kingdom (Rv 21:9 ff.).

These and so many other New Testament passages incessantly implore us modern-day Catholics to get out of our pastoral and parish ruts, to feel the energy of an evangelizing vision in the way we do church and, yes, in the way we *are* church. For no amount of business, no need of ritual, no theological assumption and no social adjustment should ever lead us to imagine that if we've taken care of our ordinary parishioners, we have done the mission of the Church.

We've taken care of our ordinary parishioners when they, as the ordinary part of their lives, become the evangelizing disciples Christ calls them to be.

# Chapter 5

# THE LARGER CONTEXT

A clear danger lurks behind any book that describes itself as a "handbook" or a "how-to" book. It's the danger of inadvertently mistaking the trees for the forest. We can become so conscious of certain objectives or certain techniques that we miss sight of the whole context in which these objectives and techniques make sense.

It's the danger of the chef who can make the soufflé, but never gets dinner complete. Or the contractor who panels a lovely basement, but never quite gets the certificate of occupancy.

This handbook deliberately looked at certain dimensions of personal and parish evangelization to provide some resources and some counterbalance to two undeniable problems on the contemporary Catholic evangelization front: that Catholics, having great resources of faith, simply do not feel themselves able to begin appropriately sharing those resources and, second, that parishes continue to overvalue their internal-organizing side to the detriment of their external-inviting side.

Chapter 2 opened up a way to look at the lives of contemporary Catholics so as to concentrate on their opportunities for personal witnessing and sharing. Chapters 3 and 4 addressed some of the explicit strategies of Goal II of the U.S. bishops' plan and strategy on evangelization, *Go and Make Disciples,* with a view to making these strategies more accessible to parishes and their leadership.

However, having looked at some of the explicit opportunities and elaborated strategies, it is time to step back and, in this final, chapter, take in the larger context of Catholic evangelization.

## *The Kingdom*

Why do Catholics care about evangelization at all? Why do we worry that the "message is not being spread," or that the "faith is not being lived"?

While it might be quite characteristic of Catholic individualism today to note that a dozen different Catholics might give a dozen different answers to these questions (and some, unfortunately, might even say that they don't care whether messages get spread or faith gets lived at all), the fundamental framework for all Catholic evangelization is the Kingdom of God.

The Kingdom of God provides the basic dynamic of Catholic evangelization. Without the Kingdom, and our adherence to it, there cannot be energy for evangelization or, indeed, for the full scope of Christian life.

Before we wrap our personal imaginations around this word *Kingdom,* with our myriad tendencies to color its image with armies, flags, trumpets and other military insignia, we need to locate ourselves in the personal imagination of Jesus Christ, for no one can doubt that the notion of the Kingdom of God was central to his life and teaching. In fact, the idea of "Kingdom" can be viewed as the central metaphor of the Gospels precisely because it was the framework, the context, out of which Jesus lived and thought.

Perhaps we can, without getting into a whole theology of

the Kingdom of God—which would be very nuanced and long—simply point to three distinct moments in the life of Jesus: the call of the first disciples, the feeding of the multitude and the commissioning of the apostles before his ascension. These three moments, lined up in a row, make a line that extends forward in time and outward in space with such universal import that they encompass our Catholic life today and point to a vision of Jesus whose vastness is the context for all evangelizing activity.

**Jesus calls the first disciples.** We can catch the essence of this scene by looking at the Gospel of Mark (Mk 1:16-20). Jesus, having just been baptized, under the power of the Holy Spirit and with the force of the vision that he received, has gone into the desert to be tested by the "Tempter." Having gone through this initial testing, Jesus emerges from the desert and proceeds to the shore of Lake Galilee. There he sees Peter and Andrew as well as James and John in the midst of the other fishermen. We need to imagine the energy, the sheer human and divine force of Jesus Christ, as he looks into the faces of these simple fishermen. In capturing that energy we begin to feel the initial opening of the Kingdom. Jesus, stopping by these four men, has begun a process of inviting them into his own experience, his own life. It's a bit like the first dividing of a fertilized cell: in this initial, personal invitation begins the public community that Jesus wants to form.

**Jesus feeds the multitude.** Hardly any other event in the life of Jesus has been recorded so broadly in all of the Gospels as this one. We might follow it in the Gospel of Luke (Lk 9:10-17). Jesus is still in Galilee, his home county, having expended enormous energy teaching, preaching and working signs. He has, pointedly, sent his Twelve Apostles out on mission themselves, as Luke tells us: "Then they set out and went from village to village proclaiming the good news and curing diseases everywhere" (Lk 9:6). It is hard to escape the feeling that Jesus sees his mission moving to a new level and this thrust by his Twelve

Apostles is bringing his work to a distinct climax. After inter-
jecting the perplexity of Herod (and raising for the reader the
crucial question: who is Jesus?), Luke narrates the scene of the
feeding of the multitude, which unfolds in the following steps.
The Twelve, returning from their mission exhausted and exhila-
rated from their work, go with Jesus to a place of rest. But the
crowds they stirred up are so great that, following after Jesus
and his band, they would not let Jesus and his disciples have
their quiet. The story line is quite clear: Jesus has used his followers to gather a crowd so vast it seems almost unfeedable;
then he, with his disciples, feeds them. In this crowd, Jesus
would seem to gather the whole of humankind; the resources
for this gathering are spelled out in the closing lines of the story:
"And when the leftover fragments were picked up, they filled
twelve wicker baskets" (Lk 9:17)—clearly saying that Jesus has
the resources to feed all who hunger. We might note, as well,
that in the next Gospel scene, Peter, having seen all this,
answers the question raised by Herod: who is Jesus? "The Messiah of God," Peter says (Lk 9:20). The Messiah is the one who
satisfies all human hunger.

**The commissioning of the disciples.** Although just
about every appearance of Jesus after his resurrection contains some dimension of sending his disciples forth,
Matthew's Gospel provides the fullest and most challenging
narration (Mt 28: 16–20). Here the eleven disciples go to a
mountain in Galilee after being ordered there by Jesus. (One
wonders if they were so reluctant that they *had* to be
ordered.) They see Jesus and fall before him in worship,
even though they have their doubts. Jesus moves close to
them (remember the moment when he first calls them?), and
we can feel the intensity of his presence. After telling them
that all authority has been given to him, he then sends them
forth to "make disciples of all nations," by baptizing them
and teaching them all that Jesus had "commanded" them.
Still stunned, the disciples then hear Jesus' final words: "And

behold, I am with you always, until the end of the age" (Mt 28:20). While it is hard to know what these Galilean fishermen and assorted friends could make of such language ("all the nations") given their own limited geographical experience, and while it is even stranger that Jesus virtually has to shove their debilitating doubts back into their faces, the whole scene transparently gives us a definite picture of the way Jesus saw his disciples and their mission. Jesus, proclaimed Messiah, having died and risen, now sends his disciples forth to the whole world.

These three moments in the life of Jesus, moments of personal invitation and powerful messianic gesturing, help frame for us the context of Catholic evangelization. They set the trajectory for the Kingdom of God. From Christ's initial calling, through the disciples in their first flushed excitement at following him, through Christ's early commissioning of his disciples to partake in his mission, then through the firstfruits of that activity, when thousands risk hunger and collapse just to hear his Word, up to this final commissioning to a universal mission—Jesus wants to reach every human being and to empower those who follow him, even in their fears and doubts, to share with him in this universal gathering.

This trajectory forms the inner dynamic of the Kingdom of God; this inner dynamic explodes in generation after generation of believers who simply cannot keep this Word to themselves, who are empowered and impelled to go out to others with the Good News of Jesus Christ. Surely that Good News will be heard differently in every era, in every culture, on every continent, through the unending multiplicity of human experience. But that Good News will not be complete until it has addressed every human heart with the same immediacy with which Jesus addressed his first disciples when he called them.

## The Vastness of the Kingdom

The three events that we have pulled from the Gospels—only a few of the many that echo the same strain—help to establish the breadth and depth of the context of Catholic evangelization.

Evangelization is constituted by the activities that continue to expand the inner and outer dynamic of the Kingdom of God. Every parish continues to find itself on that same trajectory. Every believing family in our day continues the work of peace that Jesus sent his first disciples to foster on their first mission. Every Mass, every celebration of the eucharist, continues to unveil the full meaning of the gathering of those thousands who could no longer deny their hunger. Every committed disciple forms just one more moment in which Jesus Christ, who promised that he would be with us forever, works until "the end of the age."

Once we see ourselves part of that same trajectory, the vastness of the Kingdom of God starts to become clear to us.

God gets involved in our history through Jesus Christ precisely to touch every phase of our history and every moment of human life. God becomes human through the incarnation of the Son precisely to make human history part of divine eternity. God's Spirit comes upon us exactly to accomplish the fullness that Jesus' actions and words pointed out to us: the fullness of a humankind touched by God and therefore transformed in all its relationships.

The vastness of the Kingdom of God—its universal and total scope—encircles every single evangelizing act done by a particular believer or by the community of believers, the parish. Nothing can or should hinder this Kingdom in its sweep—not because Christianity is a faith that needs to "conquer" everyone and everything else, but simply and solely because God's love will not be content until all human beings are wrapped into a communion of love that, flowing from God's inner life, has transformed human life itself.

We can make no sense of our home visiting, our mailings, our invitations, our conversations and explanations of faith unless we come to see these are part of the trajectory that Jesus, from the first moments of his ministry, set in motion.

## An Accepting Kingdom

Unfortunately, given the way Christianity has sometimes worked itself out in history, the vastness of the Kingdom can mean for some the "heavy-handedness of the Kingdom."

Rather than being seen as invitation and welcome, the Christian Word can look like one large weapon with which to slay the unbeliever or vanquish the hesitant. Jesus' injunction to "make disciples of all nations" has at times been interpreted as a ticket to stomp on all cultures for the sake of the Kingdom. There is no need to narrate those painful moments in human history when the Kingdom that should have united people in love actually divided people in hatred and blood. In spite of this, the universal claim of the Kingdom of God maintains all its force. That we, as a community of believers, proclaim God's definitive revelation in the loving Christ is neither something we should cringe over nor something we should hide. In Christ, God speaks to everyone—every person, every era, every culture.

And that may seem to create a problem. We live in a world, do we not, that prizes "pluralism" and "denominationalism" as signs of the democratic openness of its social vision. Even though the generic sameness that seems to be infecting every part of the world through good old modern marketing (until we all wear the same jeans and strut in the same tennis shoes to the rhythm of the same music) threatens to make us all the same, more and more people are insisting on their differences—and seem willing to fight for them. Distinctions, and sometimes divisions, of nationality, race, class, language and style are so prominent that sometimes they threaten the stability of national and international society. But no one can (or should) argue for their total elimination. We are different, and should be so without a bit of shame. God's Kingdom rests not on sameness but on unity.

So what can it mean to invite people into a Kingdom when diversity is so strongly prized? What does it mean to evangelize in a society that mistrusts almost all universal movements unless they are blessed by Wall Street or Walt Disney? Will not the proclamation of the Christian and Catholic faith threaten the very diversity of human cultures and religions? When does the vastness of the Kingdom mean the suffocation of all that is different?

These questions lead to questions about ecumenism and interreligious dialogue, both aspects of the vastness of the Kingdom of God. But before we can deal with them, we need to visit the first and essential assumption of Christian faith—that God's love, rather than crushing, is accepting and embracing. The only dimension of human life that God's Kingdom would eradicate is that which poisons the human enterprise at its core: sin. Apart from the evil of our hearts, Christ's love looks to cherish and accept. It is the very nature of Catholicism (which means, in its root, *for the whole*) to embrace differences into a larger unity of love.

We cannot evangelize as Catholics and Christians unless we first have this human acceptance in the very foundation of our missionary gut. Otherwise we turn the Word of God into a bully message, with unfounded threats and unloving objectives, which ultimately stifle the very point of the mission of Jesus.

## Ecumenism and Dialogue

So what do we do with ecumenism and interreligious dialogue? How do we handle diversity when proclaiming and seeking to expand the Kingdom?

Catholicism holds on to two truths: that God's message of love and forgiveness in Jesus Christ belongs to every person and that, at the same time, this message can only be imparted with love and respect.

All too often in the last thirty years the universality of Christ's message has been soft-pedaled, mostly because of the pluralistic pressures of modern life. "World mission" can look a lot like "world colonialism." All too readily today we hear, "Don't shove your faith down my throat." When that is said enough, and when the transcendent work of the Spirit is made very abstract, then the missionary impulse of the Church gets almost muted. At the same time, however, no believer can look at the results of a society without religious vision and values and see this as a good and godly thing. Around us, everywhere and everyday, the rotting fruits of an unevangelized world fill our nostrils with the unacceptable stench of wasted human life. Every one of us can document this truth by a simple reading of the daily newspaper. The major problems of modern life come from the absence of values based on the deepest human and divine truths.

God's Word, therefore, is not just an option for human life: it is the basis of human life, the foundation of human value, the starting point of human dignity, the assumption of true human community. This is why God's Word belongs to everyone in the world. As the popes have reminded us, no Christian should dare to cheat people of their right to know Jesus Christ.

Yet how does this happen? How is Christ's Word heard? How does it get translated, communicated, inculturated, made human? Only through the love and respect that every human being deserves. And that is the second truth we must hold on to, just as powerfully as the need for every person to hear the Gospel.

Some Christians—and Catholics—take evangelization as permission to dismiss and dismantle the faith and goodwill of others. Their faith gets painted in demonic colors; their differences make them into enemies to conquer. Even granting the strict words of judgment that Jesus uttered (in the context of his day), nothing in the New Testament provides a license for this kind of attitude. Again, Jesus feeds those who are hungry and invites those who are longing. That is the dynamic he began.

This dynamic actually is part of those modern movements of ecumenism and interreligious dialogue that, while maintaining the integrity of our own Catholic faith, allow us to sit with others around a table of love, based on respect, to share our message and our experience with each other. None of us can fully, or even partially, describe what the Holy Spirit is doing in the human heart and the global community. So our openness to the Spirit makes it necessary for us to share, listen, witness and invite as that is appropriate.

Many Catholics still do not know that the Christian faith of others is to be prized and respected. Without question, should God lead other Christians to seek entrance into the Church, we can only welcome them and enthusiastically celebrate. Our Christian hope says that we believe that God will lead all who believe in Christ around the same table some day—we can see this starting to happen in our own modern experience. The same faith that impels us to share with others also asks us to trust in God's continued work among the various Christian churches and communions. The ecumenical movement is part of the Spirit's evangelizing activity in the world. This hardly means that "faith makes no difference" or that "all faiths are the same." It means, rather, that God continues to work among us through our love and respect, and this no more so than among those who profess one Lord and celebrate one baptism.

Pope John Paul II has written clearly of the relationship between ecumenism and evangelization. He writes with passion: "How indeed can we proclaim the Gospel of reconciliation without at the same time being committed to working for reconciliation between Christians?...Here an imperative of charity is in question, an imperative which admits of no exception. Ecumenism is not only an internal question of the Christian communities. It is a matter of the love which God has in Jesus Christ for all humanity; to stand in the way of this love is an offense against him and against his plan to gather all people in Christ" (*Ut Unum Sint,* #98-99).

While dreams of unity color ecumenical efforts, the demands of pluralism seem to color interreligious dialogue. We might indeed imagine all Christians united, but what of Jews, Muslims, Hindus, Buddhists and so many other world faiths that do not know Christ? Is not evangelization a direct threat to them, their integrity and pluralistic rights? No one, to be particular, can be aware of the history of the Holocaust and not realize that Christian evangelization might come across to Jews as a form of genocide.

Here, too, love and respect must hold. And in love and respect, our witness to Jesus Christ will have the power that it will have. For Christ cannot be ignored by any culture or any individual person. What the encounter of Christ will come to mean in the life of a particular person depends on the Holy Spirit. That Christ can illuminate the great religious themes of these world religions is also a fruit of the Spirit's work. Our respectful and loving witness, however, means that we must approach others—in the integrity of our belief—without the conqueror's sword or the sneer of the righteous.

Paul's own struggles to reconcile his experience with his separation from his Jewish community (Rom 9–10) shows just the kind of sensitivity and openness to mystery that interreligious dialogue holds out for the Catholic Church. It is part of—and not opposed to—the vastness of the Kingdom that we still see only partly, that has not yet attained its full flowering.

### The Dream Will Not Die

*Urbi et orbi.* Translated, these words mean *for the city and the world.*

This phrase describes certain blessings and messages given at the Vatican by the Pope. At first glance, it might seem a bit arrogant. *For the city and the world?* Whose city and whose world?

Yet, once we set aside the suspicion of arrogance, these words contain a dream, one that simply will not die. It is the dream of humankind united in love, in communion, grounded on their common experience of the unifying love of God.

This is what Catholicism stands for and, symbolically, this is what Rome stands for. It has stood for this ever since, in the simple words of the Acts of the Apostles, Paul and his companions almost casually said, "And so we came to Rome" (Acts 28:14).

Rome stood for, in that ancient world, the city where all roads led and, obviously, the city from which all roads went forth. Rome stood for the heart of the human, global community, the center of human consciousness and the focus of human hopes. This clearly romanticized notion of Rome as the center is the legacy of Catholicism, even if it acknowledges other centers and the intrinsic worth of all cultures. "Rome," in this idealized sketch, stands for the dream that humans will embrace their communality insofar as our greatness, our spiritual potential, constitutes that communality.

Over the millennia, this dream has had several incarnations, the most visible one today being the basilica of St. Peter's itself. No one can walk down the Via della Conciliazione or enter the great plaza in front of St. Peter's, which Michelangelo conceived, without being stunned at the universal thrust of this spiritual edifice. In spite of the sheer immensity of the building itself, it seems to float in a weightlessness that makes it beckoning and inviting. The images of the apostles atop the basilica itself create a human dimension that is only reinforced by the two arched curves of columns that form the oval of the square. These columns are like huge arms that embrace in a single space all those in the plaza. They gather. They unite. The oval is not closed, making clear that there always seems to be room for yet more to come into the universal coming-together that the basilica represents.

The encircling plaza of St. Peter's stands at the location where tradition holds that St. Peter gave his ultimate witness, where he suffered martyrdom and was buried. The enterprising visitor to Rome can even get tickets to go deep below the structure of St. Peter's on the *scavi* tour, the excavations of the catacombs and burial sites that were situated in ancient times on what today is the Vatican. The contrast can hardly be greater—the simple stones marked with ancient lettering and the small cubicles that framed ancient graves standing as a counterbalance to the huge spaces, statues and architectural forms that make up the largest church building in the world.

Yet the connection between Peter's witness, his martyrdom (*martyros* being the Greek word for *witness*) and the gathering of vast crowds of Christians makes perfect sense, for Peter, in his death, asks every visitor to St. Peter's what is the depth of his or her faith. When Peter's martyrdom is joined with that other great witness to the faith, St. Paul, who was beheaded in Rome shortly before Peter, one can almost physically feel the apostolic foundation of the universal Church.

And what a universal Church it is, made more clearly so by the opportunities of modern travel. A visitor, standing in St. Peter's, sees people from every continent, every economic position, every occupation, every age level and every walk of life caught up in the same challenge, the same daring dream. Here humankind is embraced and faced with the mystery of Jesus' death and resurrection, here modern people must grapple with timeless teachings, here the Pentecost experience—where so many tongues cease to be an obstacle to sharing—endures as a sign for what God would bring about in the world.

This is our dream, the Catholic dream, the gathering of all into the grace of God. Evangelization today flows from that dream and, in turn, deepens and renews it. For everyone who hears Good News becomes part of the Gospel story. Everyone who encounters Christ encounters the immediacy of salvation.

Everyone who receives the Spirit is filled with the power of God to change and bring change.

Every evangelizing activity that an individual Catholic or a Catholic parish does, when done in the love and humility that Christ enjoined on his disciples, brings about in yet a fuller way the Kingdom that Jesus embodied, that he taught and lived for and that he continues to bring about through his Spirit.

# A Few Helpful Resources

CHURCH DOCUMENTS

Pope Paul VI, *On Evangelization in the Modern World* (Washington, D.C., USCC, 1975).

*To the Ends of the Earth: A Pastoral Statement on World Mission* (Washington, D.C., USCC, Nov. 12, 1986).

*Here I Am, Send Me: A Conference Response to the Evangelization of African-Americans and the National Black Catholic Pastoral Plan* (Washington, D.C., USCC, 1987).

*The National Plan for Hispanic Ministry* (Washington, D.C., USCC, 1987).

*Heritage and Hope: Evangelization in the United States* (Washington, D.C., USCC, 1991).

Pope John Paul II, *The Mission of the Redeemer: On the Permanent Validity of the Church's Missionary Mandate* (Washington, D.C., USCC, 1991).

*Go and Make Disciples: A Plan and Strategy for Catholic Evangelization in the United States* (Washington, D.C., USCC, 1993).
This is also published with a commentary and planning guide by Kenneth Boyack, C.S.P., and Frank DeSiano,

C.S.P., and is available through PNCEA (202-832-6262) and also with discussion questions and a planning process through NCCE (800-766-6223).

NATIONAL ORGANIZATIONS

Paulist National Catholic Evangelization Association (PNCEA) (202-832-6262)
Provides a varity of materials and training resources for evangelization.

National Conference for Catholic Evangelization (NCCE) (800-786-6223; 202-832-5022)
A national network of workers in evangelization; provides a range of training resources and an annual national conference.

North American Forum on the Catechumenate (202-529-9493)
Provides introductory and advanced workshops to provide skills needed for the Catechumanate; also provides workshops on "Remembering Church"—see section on ministry to inactive Catholics.

GENERAL PARISH RESOURCES

*The Evangelizing Parish: Theologies and Strategies for Renewal* (Allen, Tex., Tabor, 1987)
The classic book for introducing fundamental notions of evangelization and the parish for Catholics.

*Creating the Evangelizing Parish* by Frank DeSiano, C.S.P., and Kenneth Boyack, C.S.P. (Mahwah, Paulist Press, 1993)
A comprehensive review of parish dynamics and resources to help parishes organize for evangelization.

WELCOMING MINISTRY

*Christian Hospitality: A Handbook for Parishes* (Archdiocese of Louisville, 502-448-8581)
A collection of resources to guide parishes on many aspects of improving their welcoming ministry.

MINISTRY TO INACTIVE CATHOLICS

Landings (617-720-5986)
A small-group process of active and inactive Catholics that uses proven sharing methods to help reconcile inactive Catholics.

Remembering Church (202-529-9493)
A process that takes some of the approaches of the Catechumenate and applies them to the ministry for inactive Catholics.

*Reaching Out: A Manual for Evangelizing Inactive Catholics* (Archdiocese of Louisville, 502-448-8581)
A handy ring-bound collection of approaches and procedures for this ministry.

MAILING

*Direct Mail Ministry: Evangelism, Stewardship and Caregiving* by Walter Mueller (Nashville, Abingdon, 1989)
Although developed from an evangelical perspective, this little book contains many stimulating ideas for the ministry of mailing.

WITNESS AND SHARING

*Share Your Faith: A Behavioral Approach to Evangelization Training* by Susan Blum (Boca Raton, Jeremiah Press, 1990)
A training guide and facilitator's manual to help Catholics isolate and improve fifteen specific evangelizing behaviors.

*Discovering My Experience of God: Awareness and Witness* by Frank DeSiano, C.S.P., and Kenneth Boyack, C.S.P. (Mahwah, Paulist Press, 1992)
Helps Catholics, through a "journal" approach, discover their own story of faith and their power to communicate that story appropriately to others.

*Heart to Heart Evangelization: Building Bridges Between Proclamation and Justice* by Susan Blum Gerding, Ed.D. (Boca Raton, 1996, toll-free: 888-472-4241)
A weekend training experience for one-to-one personal evangelization provided **free** to all parishes. Transportation costs and stipends for nationally certified facilitators are offered in exchange for an opportunity to preach on behalf of the poor in the Third World. For details, contact Isaiah Ministries at the above toll-free phone number.